NON SANZ DROICT.

William Shakespeare

TWELFTH NIGHT,
or, What You Will

Edited by Herschel Baker

The Signet Classic Shakespeare
GENERAL EDITOR: SYLVAN BARNET

A SIGNET CLASSIC from
NEW AMERICAN LIBRARY
TIMES MIRROR
New York and Scarborough, Ontario
The New English Library Limited, London

SIGNET CLASSIC TRADEMARK REG. U.S. PAT. OFF. AND FOREIGN COUNTRIES
REGISTERED TRADEMARK—MARCA REGISTRADA
HECHO EN CHICAGO, U.S.A.

SIGNET, SIGNET CLASSICS, MENTOR, PLUME AND MERIDIAN BOOKS
are published in the United States by
The New American Library, Inc.,
1301 Avenue of the Americas, New York, New York 10019,
in Canada by The New American Library of Canada Limited,
81 Mack Avenue, Scarborough, 704, Ontario,
in the United Kingdom by The New English Library Limited,
Barnard's Inn, Holborn, London, E.C. 1, England.

First Printing, June, 1965

9 10 11 12 13 14 15 16 17

PRINTED IN THE UNITED STATES OF AMERICA

Contents

Shakespeare: Prefatory Remarks

Between the record of his baptism in Stratford on 26 April 1564 and the record of his burial in Stratford on 25 April 1616, some forty documents name Shakespeare, and many others name his parents, his children, and his grandchildren. More facts are known about William Shakespeare than about any other playwright of the period except Ben Jonson. The facts should, however, be distinguished from the legends. The latter, inevitably more engaging and better known, tell us that the Stratford boy killed a calf in high style, poached deer and rabbits, and was forced to flee to London, where he held horses outside a playhouse. These traditions are only traditions; they may be true, but no evidence supports them, and it is well to stick to the facts.

Mary Arden, the dramatist's mother, was the daughter of a substantial landowner; about 1557 she married John Shakespeare, who was a glove-maker and trader in various farm commodities. In 1557 John Shakespeare was a member of the Council (the governing body of Stratford), in 1558 a constable of the borough, in 1561 one of the two town chamberlains, in 1565 an alderman (entitling him to the appellation "Mr."), in 1568 high bailiff—the town's highest political office, equivalent to mayor. After 1577, for an unknown reason he drops out of local politics. The birthday of William Shakespeare, the eldest son of this locally prominent man, is unrecorded; but the Stratford parish register records that the infant was baptized on 26 April 1564. (It is quite possible that he was born on 23

April, but this date has probably been assigned by tradition because it is the date on which, fifty-two years later, he died.) The attendance records of the Stratford grammar school of the period are not extant, but it is reasonable to assume that the son of a local official attended the school and received substantial training in Latin. The masters of the school from Shakespeare's seventh to fifteenth years held Oxford degrees; the Elizabethan curriculum excluded mathematics and the natural sciences but taught a good deal of Latin rhetoric, logic, and literature. On 27 November 1582 a marriage license was issued to Shakespeare and Anne Hathaway, eight years his senior. The couple had a child in May, 1583. Perhaps the marriage was necessary, but perhaps the couple had earlier engaged in a formal "troth plight" which would render their children legitimate even if no further ceremony were performed. In 1585 Anne Hathaway bore Shakespeare twins.

That Shakespeare was born is excellent; that he married and had children is pleasant; but that we know nothing about his departure from Stratford to London, or about the beginning of his theatrical career, is lamentable and must be admitted. We would gladly sacrifice details about his children's baptism for details about his earliest days on the stage. Perhaps the poaching episode is true (but it is first reported almost a century after Shakespeare's death), or perhaps he first left Stratford to be a schoolteacher, as another tradition holds; perhaps he was moved by

> Such wind as scatters young men through the world,
> To seek their fortunes further than at home
> Where small experience grows.

In 1592, thanks to the cantankerousness of Robert Greene, a rival playwright and a pamphleteer, we have our first reference, a snarling one, to Shakespeare as an actor and playwright. Greene warns those of his own educated friends who wrote for the theater against an actor who has presumed to turn playwright:

There is an upstart crow, beautified with our feathers, that with his *tiger's heart wrapped in a player's hide* supposes he is as well able to bombast out a blank verse as the best of you, and being an absolute Johannes-factotum is in his own conceit the only Shake-scene in a country.

The reference to the player, as well as the allusion to Aesop's crow (who strutted in borrowed plumage, as an actor struts in fine words not his own), makes it clear that by this date Shakespeare had both acted and written. That Shakespeare is meant is indicated not only by "Shake-scene" but by the parody of a line from one of Shakespeare's plays, *3 Henry VI:* "O, tiger's heart wrapped in a woman's hide." If Shakespeare in 1592 was prominent enough to be attacked by an envious dramatist, he probably had served an apprenticeship in the theater for at least a few years.

In any case, by 1592 Shakespeare had acted and written, and there are a number of subsequent references to him as an actor: documents indicate that in 1598 he is a "principal comedian," in 1603 a "principal tragedian," in 1608 he is one of the "men players." The profession of actor was not for a gentleman, and it occasionally drew the scorn of university men who resented writing speeches for persons less educated than themselves, but it was respectable enough: players, if prosperous, were in effect members of the bourgeoisie, and there is nothing to suggest that Stratford considered William Shakespeare less than a solid citizen. When, in 1596, the Shakespeares were granted a coat of arms, the grant was made to Shakespeare's father, but probably William Shakespeare (who the next year bought the second-largest house in town) had arranged the matter on his own behalf. In subsequent transactions he is occasionally styled a gentleman.

Although in 1593 and 1594 Shakespeare published two narrative poems dedicated to the Earl of Southampton, *Venus and Adonis* and *The Rape of Lucrece,* and may well have written most or all of his sonnets in the middle nineties, Shakespeare's literary activity seems to have been almost entirely devoted to the theater. (It may be significant that the two narrative poems were written in years when the plague closed the theaters for several months.) In 1594 he was a charter member of a theatrical company called the Chamberlain's Men (which in 1603 changed its name to the King's Men); until he retired to Stratford (about 1611, apparently), he was with this remarkably stable company. From 1599 the company acted primarily at the Globe Theatre, in which Shakespeare held a one-tenth interest. Other Elizabethan dramatists are known to have acted, but no other is known also to have been entitled to a share in the profits of the playhouse.

Shakespeare's first eight published plays did not have his name on them, but this is not remarkable; the most popular play of the sixteenth century, Thomas Kyd's *The Spanish Tragedy,* went through many editions without naming Kyd, and Kyd's authorship is known only because a book on the profession of acting happens to quote (and attribute to Kyd) some lines on the interest of Roman emperors in the drama. What is remarkable is that after 1598 Shakespeare's name commonly appears on printed plays—some of which are not his. Another indication of his popularity comes from Francis Meres, author of *Palladis Tamia: Wit's Treasury* (1598): in this anthology of snippets accompanied by an essay on literature, many playwrights are mentioned, but Shakespeare's name occurs more often than any other, and Shakespeare is the only playwright whose plays are listed.

From his acting, playwriting, and share in a theater, Shakespeare seems to have made considerable money. He put it to work, making substantial investments in Stratford real estate. When he made his will (less than a month before he died), he sought to leave his property intact to his descendants. Of small bequests to relatives and to friends (including three actors, Richard Burbage, John Heminges, and Henry Condell), that to his wife of the second-best bed has provoked the most comment; perhaps it was the bed the couple had slept in, the best being reserved for visitors. In any case, had Shakespeare not excepted it, the bed would have gone (with the rest of his household possessions) to his daughter and her husband. On 25 April 1616 he was buried within the chancel of the church at Stratford. An unattractive monument to his memory, placed on a wall near the grave, says he died on 23 April. Over the grave itself are the lines, perhaps by Shakespeare, that (more than his literary fame) have kept his bones undisturbed in the crowded burial ground where old bones were often dislodged to make way for new:

> Good friend, for Jesus' sake forbear
> To dig the dust enclosèd here.
> Blessed be the man that spares these stones
> And cursed be he that moves my bones.

Thirty-seven plays, as well as some nondramatic poems, are held to constitute the Shakespeare canon. The dates of composition of most of the works are highly uncertain, but there is often evidence of a *terminus a quo* (starting point) and/or a *terminus ad quem* (terminal point) that provides a framework for intelligent guessing. For example, *Richard II* cannot be earlier than 1595, the publication date of some material to which it is indebted; *The Merchant of Venice* cannot be later than 1598, the year Francis Meres mentioned it. Sometimes arguments for a date hang on an alleged topical allusion, such as the lines about the unseasonable weather in *A Midsummer Night's Dream,* II.i.81–117, but such an allusion (if indeed it is an allusion) can be variously interpreted, and in any case there is always the possibility that a topical allusion was inserted during a revision, years after the composition of a play. Dates are often attributed on the basis of style, and although conjectures about style usually rest on other conjectures, sooner or later one must rely on one's literary sense. There is no real proof, for example, that *Othello* is not as early as *Romeo and Juliet,* but one feels *Othello* is later, and because the first record of its performance is 1604, one is glad enough to set its composition at that date and not push it back into Shakespeare's early years. The following chronology, then, is as much indebted to informed guesswork and sensitivity as it is to fact. The dates, necessarily imprecise, indicate something like a scholarly consensus.

PLAYS

1588–93	*The Comedy of Errors*
1588–94	*Love's Labor's Lost*
1590–91	*2 Henry VI*
1590–91	*3 Henry VI*
1591–92	*1 Henry VI*
1592–93	*Richard III*
1592–94	*Titus Andronicus*
1593–94	*The Taming of the Shrew*
1593–95	*The Two Gentlemen of Verona*
1594–96	*Romeo and Juliet*
1595	*Richard II*
1594–96	*A Midsummer Night's Dream*
1596–97	*King John*
1596–97	*The Merchant of Venice*
1597	*1 Henry IV*
1597–98	*2 Henry IV*
1598–1600	*Much Ado About Nothing*
1598–99	*Henry V*
1599	*Julius Caesar*
1599–1600	*As You Like It*
1599–1600	*Twelfth Night*
1600–01	*Hamlet*
1597–1601	*The Merry Wives of Windsor*
1601–02	*Troilus and Cressida*
1602–04	*All's Well That Ends Well*
1603–04	*Othello*
1604	*Measure for Measure*
1605–06	*King Lear*
1605–06	*Macbeth*
1606–07	*Antony and Cleopatra*
1605–08	*Timon of Athens*
1607–09	*Coriolanus*
1608	*Pericles*

1609–10	*Cymbeline*
1610–11	*The Winter's Tale*
1611	*The Tempest*
1612–13	*Henry VIII*

POEMS

1592	*Venus and Adonis*
1593–94	*The Rape of Lucrece*
1593–1600	*Sonnets*
1600–01	*The Phoenix and the Turtle*

Shakespeare's Theater

In Shakespeare's infancy, Elizabethan actors performed wherever they could—in great halls, at court, in the courtyards of inns. The innyards must have made rather unsatisfactory theaters: on some days they were unavailable because carters bringing goods to London used them as depots; when available, they had to be rented from the innkeeper; perhaps most important, London inns were subject to the Common Council of London, which was not well disposed toward theatricals. In 1574 the Common Council required that plays and playing places in London be licensed. It asserted that

> sundry great disorders and inconveniences have been found to ensue to this city by the inordinate haunting of great multitudes of people, specially youth, to plays, interludes, and shows, namely occasion of frays and quarrels, evil practices of incontinency in great inns having chambers and secret places adjoining to their open stages and galleries,

and ordered that innkeepers who wished licenses to hold performances put up a bond and make contributions to the poor.

The requirement that plays and innyard theaters be licensed, along with the other drawbacks of playing at inns, probably drove James Burbage (a carpenter-turned-actor) to rent in 1576 a plot of land northeast of the city walls and to build here—on property outside the jurisdiction of the city—England's first permanent construction designed for plays. He called it simply the Theatre. About all that is known of its construction is that it was wood. It soon had imitators, the most famous being the Globe (1599), built across the Thames (again outside the city's jurisdiction), out of timbers of the Theatre, which had been dismantled when Burbage's lease ran out.

There are three important sources of information about the structure of Elizabethan playhouses—drawings, a contract, and stage directions in plays. Of drawings, only the so-called De Witt drawing (c. 1596) of the Swan—really a friend's copy of De Witt's drawing—is of much significance. It shows a building of three tiers, with a stage jutting from a wall into the yard or center of the building. The tiers are roofed, and part of the stage is covered by a roof that projects from the rear and is supported at its front on two posts, but the groundlings, who paid a penny to stand in front of the stage, were exposed to the sky. (Performances in such a playhouse were held only in the daytime; artificial illumination was not used.) At the rear of the stage are two doors; above the stage is a gallery. The second major source of information, the contract for the Fortune, specifies that although the Globe is to be the model, the Fortune is to be square, eighty feet outside and fifty-five inside. The stage is to be forty-three feet broad, and is to extend into the middle of the yard (i.e., it is twenty-seven and a half feet deep). For patrons willing to pay more than the general admission charged of the groundlings, there were to be three galleries provided with seats. From the third chief source, stage directions, one learns that entrance to the stage was by doors, presumably spaced widely apart at the rear ("Enter one citizen at one door, and another at the other"), and that in addition to the platform stage there was occasionally some sort of curtained booth or alcove allowing for "discovery" scenes, and some sort of play-

ing space "aloft" or "above" to represent (for example)
the top of a city's walls or a room above the street. Doubtless each theater had its own peculiarities, but perhaps
we can talk about a "typical" Elizabethan theater if we
realize that no theater need exactly have fit the descrip-
tion, just as no father is the typical father with 3.7 children.
This hypothetical theater is wooden, round or polygonal
(in *Henry V* Shakespeare calls it a "wooden *O*"), capable
of holding some eight hundred spectators standing in the
yard around the projecting elevated stage and some fifteen
hundred additional spectators seated in the three roofed
galleries. The stage, protected by a "shadow" or "heavens"
or roof, is entered by two doors; behind the doors is the
"tiring house" (attiring house, i.e., dressing room), and
above the doors is some sort of gallery that may sometimes hold spectators but that can be used (for example)
as the bedroom from which Romeo—according to a stage
direction in one text—"goeth down." Some evidence suggests that a throne can be lowered onto the platform stage,
perhaps from the "shadow"; certainly characters can de-
scend from the stage through a trap or traps into the cellar
or "hell." Sometimes this space beneath the platform
accommodates a sound-effects man or musician (in *Antony
and Cleopatra* "music of the hautboys is under the stage")
or an actor (in *Hamlet* the "Ghost cries under the stage").
Most characters simply walk on and off, but because there
is no curtain in front of the platform, corpses will have
to be carried off (Hamlet must lug Polonius' guts into
the neighbor room), or will have to fall at the rear, where
the curtain on the alcove or booth can be drawn to conceal them.

Such may have been the so-called "public theater."
Another kind of theater, called the "private theater" because its much greater admission charge limited its audience to the wealthy or the prodigal, must be briefly
mentioned. The private theater was basically a large room,
entirely roofed and therefore artificially illuminated, with
a stage at one end. In 1576 one such theater was established in Blackfriars, a Dominican priory in London that
had been suppressed in 1538 and confiscated by the

Crown and thus was not under the city's jurisdiction. All the actors in the Blackfriars theater were boys about eight to thirteen years old (in the public theaters similar boys played female parts; a boy Lady Macbeth played to a man Macbeth). This private theater had a precarious existence, and ceased operations in 1584. In 1596 James Burbage, who had already made theatrical history by building the Theatre, began to construct a second Blackfriars theater. He died in 1597, and for several years this second Blackfriars theater was used by a troupe of boys, but in 1608 two of Burbage's sons and five other actors (including Shakespeare) became joint operators of the theater, using it in the winter when the open-air Globe was unsuitable. Perhaps such a smaller theater, roofed, artificially illuminated, and with a tradition of a courtly audience, exerted an influence on Shakespeare's late plays.

Performances in the private theaters may well have had intermissions during which music was played, but in the public theaters the action was probably uninterrupted, flowing from scene to scene almost without a break. Actors would enter, speak, exit, and others would immediately enter and establish (if necessary) the new locale by a few properties and by words and gestures. Here are some samples of Shakespeare's scene painting:

> This is Illyria, lady.

> Well, this is the Forest of Arden.

> This castle hath a pleasant seat; the air
> Nimbly and sweetly recommends itself
> Unto our gentle senses.

On the other hand, it is a mistake to conceive of the Elizabethan stage as bare. Although Shakespeare's Chorus in *Henry V* calls the stage an "unworthy scaffold" and urges the spectators to "eke out our performance with your mind," there was considerable spectacle. The last act of *Macbeth,* for example, has five stage directions calling for "drum and colors," and another sort of appeal to the eye is indicated by the stage direction "Enter Macduff, with Macbeth's head." Some scenery and properties may have been substantial; doubtless a throne was used, and in one play of the period we encounter this direction: "Hector takes up a great piece of rock and casts at Ajax, who tears up a young tree by the roots and assails Hector." The matter is of some importance, and will be glanced at again in the next section.

The Texts of Shakespeare

Though eighteen of his plays were published during his lifetime, Shakespeare seems never to have supervised their publication. There is nothing unusual here; when a playwright sold a play to a theatrical company he surrendered his ownership of it. Normally a company would not publish the play, because to publish it meant to allow competitors to acquire the piece. Some plays, however, did get published: apparently treacherous actors sometimes pieced together a play for a publisher, sometimes a company in need of money sold a play, and sometimes a company allowed a play to be published that no longer drew audiences. That Shakespeare did not concern himself with publication, then, is scarcely remarkable; of his contemporaries only Ben Jonson carefully supervised the publication of his own plays. In 1623, seven years after Shakespeare's death, John Heminges and Henry Condell (two senior members of Shakespeare's company, who had performed with him for about twenty years) collected his plays—published and unpublished—into a large volume, commonly called the First Folio. (A folio is a volume consisting of sheets that have been folded once, each sheet thus making two leaves, or four pages. The eighteen plays published during Shakespeare's lifetime had been issued one play per volume in small books call quartos. Each sheet in a quarto has been folded twice, making four leaves, or eight pages.) The First Folio contains thirty-six plays; a thirty-seventh, *Pericles,* though not in the Folio is regarded as canonical. Heminges and Condell suggest in an address "To the great variety of readers" that the republished plays are presented in better form than in the quartos: "Before you were abused with diverse stolen and surreptitious copies, maimed and deformed by the frauds and stealths of injurious impostors that exposed them; even those, are now offered to your view cured and perfect of their limbs, and all the rest absolute in their numbers, as he [i.e., Shakespeare] conceived them."

Whoever was assigned to prepare the texts for publication in the First Folio seems to have taken his job seriously and yet not to have performed it with uniform care. The sources of the texts seem to have been, in general, good unpublished copies or the best published copies. The first play in the collection, *The Tempest,* is divided into acts and scenes, has unusually full stage directions and descriptions of spectacle, and concludes with a list of the characters, but the editor was not able (or willing) to present all of the succeeding texts so fully dressed. Later texts occasionally show signs of carelessness: in one scene of *Much Ado About Nothing* the names of actors, instead of characters, appear as speech prefixes, as they had in the quarto, which the Folio reprints; proofreading throughout the Folio is spotty and apparently was done without reference to the printer's copy; the pagination of *Hamlet* jumps from 156 to 257.

A modern editor of Shakespeare must first select his copy; no problem if the play exists only in the Folio, but a considerable problem if the relationship between a quarto and the Folio—or an early quarto and a later one—is unclear. When an editor has chosen what seems to him to be the most authoritative text or texts for his copy, he has not done with making decisions. First of all, he must reckon with Elizabethan spelling. If he is not producing a facsimile, he probably modernizes it, but ought he to preserve the old form of words that apparently were pronounced quite unlike their modern forms—"lanthorn," "alablaster"? If he preserves these forms, is he really preserving Shakespeare's forms or perhaps those of a compositor in the printing house? What is one to do when one finds "lanthorn" and "lantern" in adjacent lines? (The editors of this series in general, but not invariably, assume that words should be spelled in their modern form.) Elizabethan punctuation, too, presents problems. For example in the First Folio, the only text for the play, Macbeth rejects his wife's idea that he can wash the blood from his hand:

> no: this my Hand will rather
> The multitudinous Seas incarnadine,
> Making the Greene one, Red.

Obviously an editor will remove the superfluous capitals, and he will probably alter the spelling to "incarnadine," but will he leave the comma before "red," letting Macbeth speak of the sea as "the green one," or will he (like most modern editors) remove the comma and thus have Macbeth say that his hand will make the ocean *uniformly* red?

An editor will sometimes have to change more than spelling or punctuation. Macbeth says to his wife:

> I dare do all that may become a man,
> Who dares no more, is none.

For two centuries editors have agreed that the second line is unsatisfactory, and have emended "no" to "do": "Who dares do more is none." But when in the same play Ross says that fearful persons

> floate vpon a wilde and violent Sea
> Each way, and moue,

need "move" be emended to "none," as it often is, on the hunch that the compositor misread the manuscript? The editors of the Signet Classic Shakespeare have restrained themselves from making abundant emendations. In their minds they hear Dr. Johnson on the dangers of emending: "I have adopted the Roman sentiment, that it is more honorable to save a citizen than to kill an enemy." Some departures (in addition to spelling, punctuation, and lineation) from the copy text have of course been made, but the original readings are listed in a note following the play, so that the reader can evaluate them for himself.

The editors of the Signet Classic Shakespeare, following tradition, have added line numbers and in many cases act and scene divisions as well as indications of locale at the beginning of scenes. The Folio divided most of the plays into acts and some into scenes. Early eighteenth-century editors increased the divisions. These divisions, which provide a convenient way of referring to passages in the plays, have been retained, but when not in the text chosen as the basis for the Signet Classic text they are enclosed in square brackets [ ] to indicate that they are editorial additions. Similarly, although no play of Shakespeare's published during his lifetime was equipped with indications of locale at the heads of scene divisions, locales have here been added in square brackets for the convenience of the reader, who lacks the information afforded to spectators by costumes, properties, and gestures. The spectator can tell at a glance he is in the throne room, but without an editorial indication the reader may be puzzled for a while. It should be mentioned, incidentally, that there are a few authentic stage directions —perhaps Shakespeare's, perhaps a prompter's—that suggest locales: for example, "Enter Brutus in his orchard," and "They go up into the Senate house." It is hoped that the bracketed additions provide the reader with the sort of help provided in these two authentic directions, but it is equally hoped that the reader will remember that the stage was not loaded with scenery.

No editor during the course of his work can fail to recollect some words Heminges and Condell prefixed to the Folio:

It had been a thing, we confess, worthy to have been wished, that the author himself had lived to have set forth and overseen his own writings. But since it hath been ordained otherwise, and he by death departed from that right, we pray you do not envy his friends the office of their care and pain to have collected and published them.

Nor can an editor, after he has done his best, forget Heminges and Condell's final words: "And so we leave you to other of his friends, whom if you need can be your guides. If you need them not, you can lead yourselves, and others. And such readers we wish him."

SYLVAN BARNET
Tufts University

Introduction

Twelfth Night is such a genial, charming play that for a certain kind of reader its charm is self-defeating. Johnson, for example, admired its elegance and ease and its exquisite humor, and he conceded that it might be diverting on the stage; but because the principal action "wants credibility" and "exhibits no just picture of life," he remarked with disapproval, it cannot be instructive or tell us anything important. In short, it fails the test of relevance.

This great critic's cold opinion of the most profound of Shakespeare's so-called "golden comedies" presents us with a hard decision: either to dismiss *Twelfth Night* as false and fatuous or to accept it as a version of romance— deft and entertaining, to be sure, but remote from our concerns and exempt from any common-sense appraisal. As usual, Johnson, a man not given to unconsidered judgments, seems to argue from the facts. For one thing, what we know or may infer about the circumstances of its first production would indicate that *Twelfth Night* was conceived and written as a kind of bagatelle. If, as many scholars think, it was commissioned for performance by the fledgling lawyers of the Middle Temple at the romp that crowned their Christmas celebration, the play was tailored to an annual frolic when duty and convention were ignored, and when, in a saturnalian Feast of Misrule, mirth became the order of the day. Even the subtitle—*What You Will*—repudiates, or so it seems, the drab and probable for the promise of the unexpected.[1] Life, as most men come to know it, is a frayed and tattered thing of unexpressed desires and disappointed hopes, and its tumults rarely find repose. In the world depicted by *Twelfth Night*, however, it would seem that perturbation leads to calm and all suspensions are resolved, so that by happy if implausible coincidence afflicted virtue is rewarded, folly is exposed, and error yields to knowledge.

The ingredients of this consoling fiction are the staple items of romance: shipwreck, alienation, and wandering in a remote realm where a pair of high-born lovers melodiously indulge a set of attitudes untested by experience, where a maiden in distress by luck and pluck gets everything she wants, and where the pretensions of an "affectioned ass" are demolished by a pack of gay tormentors. The main plot, articulated by the ancient devices of disguise and mistaken identity, presents a love story (or a brace of interlocking love stories) that leads through skillful convolutions to a final recognition scene; and the subplot—a kind of anti-masque—involves the "lighter people" in a complicated jest. Finally, all these knotted strands of action are conducted in a language so precise that form and function seem to coincide, with Orsino's artful "fancy" and Viola's deep but muted love as charmingly conveyed as Sir Toby's burly humor and the wit and music of the Clown.

Indeed, this play, which starts and ends with music,

---

[1] Despite Leslie Hotson's interesting attempt in *The First Night of Twelfth Night* (1954) to show that the play was commissioned for performance before the Queen and court at Whitehall on Twelfth Night (January 6) in 1601 to celebrate the splendid visit of Virginio Orsini, Duke of Bracchiano, most scholars still accept an entry of February 2, 1602, in the diary of John Manningham, a barrister of the Middle Temple, as pointing to its first production in the Middle Temple hall on Twelfth Night of that year: "At our feast we had a play called *Twelve Night, or What You Will*, much like the *Comedy of Errors* or *Menechmi* in Plautus, but most like and near to that in Italian called *Inganni*. A good practice in it to make the steward believe his Lady widow was in love with him, by counterfeiting a letter as from his Lady in general terms, telling him what she liked best in him, and prescribing his gesture in smiling, his apparel, etc., and then when he came to practice making him believe they took him to be mad." On Manningham's clever guess about Nicolò Secchi's *Inganni*, see "The Source of *Twelfth Night*," pp. 141–42.

and which is studded with so many lovely songs, might be said to approach the condition of that art where form and style are everything, and where there is, or should be, no appeal to values and criteria not inherent in the work itself. In more severely imitative kinds of art, the reverse, of course, is true. Because Holbein's portrait of Sir Thomas More or Richardson's *Clarissa*—which, incidentally, was one of Johnson's favorite books—seek in different, complicated ways to represent contemporary experience with fidelity, at least a part of our response to them is based on what we know of life, and therefore we require that they express some aspect of the truth about the things they represent. On the other hand, a Mozart serenade stands for nothing but itself; it has a logic of its own, and it creates an independent frame of reference that baffles any moral or utilitarian test. *Twelfth Night* is not this kind of work, of course, but it is such a triumph of artifice and style, and shows such mastery of convention, that some readers might regard it as a self-subsistent artifact, or, at any rate, as a work invulnerable to the expectations and probabilities derived from everyday experience. Beguiled by its mazy plot and music, they would not even dare to ask if it is "true." For them, therefore, Johnson's test of relevance would appear to be irrelevant, and his common-sense, adverse opinion merely an impertinence.

To regard *Twelfth Night* either as escapist folderol or adroit but meaningless romance is, however, to forget its function as a play. But since it is a play, and since a play, as Aristotle said, is the imitation of an action, it must meet the test of relevance. This test can never be evaded in a literary production, because no true work of literature ignores what Johnson means by "life," and no honest writer, however much concerned with form and style, neglects his only proper subject, which is the human situation. It is not that we require an easy calculus of triumph for the good and disaster for the bad, but that a play reveal—or permit us to infer—a necessary connection between what happens to a man and the kind of man he is. When this requirement is evaded, as it seems to be evaded, for example, in the last act of *Measure for Measure,* we are baffled and uneasy because we feel a lack of moral sequence. Conversely, when the conduct of the action, however painful, satisfies our moral expectations we are forced to yield assent. Thus, although the conclusion of *King Lear* is as harrowing as anything in drama, we accept it, in our anguish, because we recognize its dreadful logic.

We do not look for dreadful logic in *Twelfth Night,* of course, but we do expect to find a real connection between its artful, entertaining fiction and those aspects of experience that it seeks to represent. We expect to find some reference, even if oblique and stylized, to the world which each of us inhabits—a refinement of our own perceptions, an enlargement of our knowledge or compassion, a demonstration of how men and women act, and why. Otherwise art deteriorates to mere technique, and literature becomes gesticulation.

What, then, is there in *Twelfth Night* to save it from this danger? For one thing, there is a shaping theme that enables us to view the conventions of romance as a paradigm of our own behavior; for another, there is, in the subplot, such skillful use of sharp and even topical detail in depicting various kinds of folly that the effect is almost photographic. These two features of the work remove it from the realm of pure romance and attach it to our own experience. They remind us that despite its old-fashioned apparatus, its lyric grace, and what Johnson called its lack of "credibility," *Twelfth Night* should not be thought of as a piece of music or as an empty virtuoso exercise in style, but as a play that we may verify by what we know of life.

Twelfth Night meets this test with ease, for it concerns a basic human problem; or, if that sounds too severe for such a gay and sprightly work of art, it records and comments on a mode of human action that all men everywhere exhibit. This might be defined as our native bent for self-deception, or, conversely, as our difficulty in achieving self-awareness. Here the theme is given comic statement and presented as romance, but it has a universal application. Is it possible, *Twelfth Night* makes us wonder, for us to know the truth about ourselves? And even if we gain such knowledge, Shakespeare asks in other, darker plays, can such knowledge be endured? We see these questions posed when Richard II, stripped of crown and power and even of his misconceptions, sits in Pomfret Castle and explores his final, humbling recognition of himself; when Henry V, on the eve of Agincourt, expounds the wide distinction between the common notion of a king and the kingly burden that he bears; when Othello is compelled to face the horror of the deed he did "in honor"; when Lear tears off his clothing to reveal the "unaccommodated man." Such analogues in plays so different from *Twelfth Night* suggest how often, and in what varied contexts, Shakespeare used the theme. For him—as for Sophocles and Pirandello—to show one's growth toward self-awareness is almost coextensive with the art of drama.

This theme, so massive and protean, receives consummate comic statement in *Twelfth Night*. Here Shakespeare has to trim it not merely to the comic form (which requires a complex plot directed toward a happy ending) but also, presumably, to the interests of a special clientele—the debonair young lawyers at their revels in the Middle Temple. Almost inevitably, therefore, he writes a play of love: not love as the annihilating passion shared by Romeo and Juliet or the febrile lust of Troilus, but as a mode of social intercourse that works its way through opposition to eventual satisfaction. He had done this sort of thing before, of course, in such plays as *The Two Gentlemen of Verona* and *As You Like It*; but in *Twelfth Night* he makes a signal innovation, for here the lovers' triumph is delayed not by the customary impediments of parental disapproval or insolvency or politics, but by their own deceits and self-deceptions. To secure this innovation he manipulates the old conventions of romance—notably the stock devices of disguise and mistaken identity—not merely that they might complicate the action and so provide diversion but that they might serve almost as metaphors or emblems for mental obfuscation. The perplexity of the plot—where, among many other sources of confusion, a girl disguised as a boy loves a man who commissions her to woo a lady whose advances she must check—represents in concrete terms the intellectual and emotional bewilderment that almost every character in the play exhibits. As a consequence, the machinery of romance acquires the novel function of articulating theme. To be sure, the convolutions of the plot provide diversion of a sort, but they also bind the characters in a web of interwoven error, and thus they underscore the meaning of the play: that most men never know, and maybe never have a chance to know, the truth about themselves.

But if, as the knotty and perplexing plot suggests, men are forced by circumstances into compounded misconceptions, they are also trapped by their illusions. Between the errors thrust upon them and those they generate themselves, they are caught as in a vise—victims not merely of deceit but also of their own folly. Orsino, for example, though

> Of great estate, of fresh and stainless youth;
> In voices well divulged, free, learned, and valiant,
> And in dimension and the shape of nature
> A gracious person,

is in fact so blinded by his image of himself as an ardent but despairing lover that he is maimed by his obsession. We see him first as he indulges this obsession with his famous speech on music as the food of love, and this speech, however lovely to the ear, reveals the speaker as a narcissistic fool. Much given to discussions about his complicated states of mind, he, like most self-centered persons, is really very simple. Whereas he tells Viola that

> such as I am all true lovers are,
> Unstaid and skittish in all motions else
> Save in the constant image of the creature
> That is beloved,

the only thing he loves is his romantic notion of the lover that he himself exemplifies, and he finds it so appealing that he never even asks if it is true. He leaves the play as he had entered it, with highfalutin talk about his "fancy," but this "fancy" is no more to be confused with love than his lyric self-descriptions are to be confused with fact. His soft, unmanly pleasure in caressing his emotions, his delight in "old and antic" songs as a solace for his "passion," even his petulant threat of violence against Olivia and "Cesario" for their presumed unfaithfulness reveal the sentimentalist who prefers the comfort of his own illusions to the dangers of candid self-appraisal.

In varying degrees, almost all the other characters in the play are shackled by their inability or refusal to comprehend their own emotions, or even to discern their blunders. Olivia's preoccupation with "a brother's dead love" is so unreal that a single visit from "Cesario" is enough to shatter it—and to provide her with a new obsession that is even more absurd, because it rests upon a yet more rudimentary error. Malvolio, "sick of self-love," is so easily led to self-exposure and humiliation that even as we laugh we pity him: "Alas, poor fool, how have they baffled thee!" Sir Andrew's imposing list of follies, both natural and acquired, makes him everybody's fool; and although Sir Toby has a searching eye for other people's foibles, he is usually much too drunk to recognize his own. Even Viola, who at least is in possession of the facts that save her from Olivia's type of blunder, thinks she must embark upon a program of deceit in order to survive. "Conceal me what I am," she tells the captain,

> and be my aid
> For such disguise as haply shall become
> The form of my intent.

Her finest moment in the play—the speech about the love-lorn girl who never told her love—is charming and pathetic, but it shows a certain pleasure in equivocation. Indeed, her skill and relish for the kind of organized deceit on which the action hangs are appropriate for the heroine of a play in which dissimulation and deception are routine. Only the Clown, it seems, is clear-eyed and wise enough to stand somewhat above the antics of the others and to comment on their follies. Knowing that foolery "does walk about the orb like the sun," he is as quick to puncture Orsino's egomania as to expose Olivia's silly posture of bereavement; and it is he, in the amusing but disturbing interview with the "lunatic" Malvolio, who makes us trace the narrow line between the madman and the sage. The Clown alone is immune to the pandemic error in Illyria—but he must wear a mask against contagion and infection, and he must hide his wisdom as the babble of a licensed fool. In a world where everyone is slightly mad, his motley is a badge of knowledge.

Finally, the plotting, which Johnson found offensive, is also made to demonstrate the fact that most men live by error and illusion. The three main lines of action—Orsino's languid courtship of Olivia, Olivia's imbroglio with Viola and Sebastian, and Malvolio's disgrace—do not appear as isolated plots that run their parallel and independent courses; they come to us instead as reciprocal and reverberating statements of a single situation, which is the gulling of a fool. Writers from Aristophanes to Shaw have used this situation, in one form or another, to pedagogic purpose, for they have brought the gull through ridicule to exposure and correction. It is significant that although Orsino, Olivia, and Malvolio are all the victims of deception fostered either by themselves or others, they learn nothing from experience. Two of them are unmolested in their folly, and the third, though harshly treated, clings to his absurd illusions. Malvolio's credulity —which is no sillier than that which goes unpunished in his betters—is chastised so severely that he becomes, as Lamb observed, an almost tragic figure; but Orsino and Olivia are never even chided. None of them is changed, however, and none surrenders his obsession. The denouement affords a kind of liberation, to be sure, for the proper pairing off of lovers signifies release from labyrinthine misconception. But the ease with which Orsino shifts his "fancy" from Olivia to Viola matches that with which, earlier, Olivia turns from anchorite to ardent lover and then substitutes Sebastian for "Cesario." Neither of these self-indulgent egotists has been compelled to shake off his illusion, and in a sense, therefore, neither earns the triumph he enjoys. Perhaps, as Johnson thought, Sir Andrew's "natural fatuity" renders him ineligible for comic therapy, but at any rate he stays, as he will always stay, a fool. Sir Toby, too, remains what he had been before—a sot and parasite—and in addition he acquires Maria. As for Malvolio, he not only profits nothing from his hard instruction, but as he takes his angry leave we see his self-love stiffened by his sense of injured merit. "I'll be revenged on the whole pack of you," he snarls as he departs.

Hazlitt thought that Shakespeare was "too good-natured and magnanimous" to treat his comic knaves and fools as they deserve. Perhaps for this reason or perhaps because he makes us recognize ourselves in them, we are glad for these deluded people in Illyria, for they teach us what, alas, we need to know: that since we rarely win our way to truth, we must settle for illusion.

HERSCHEL BAKER
Harvard University

Twelfth Night,
or, What You Will.

Orsino, Duke of Illyria
Sebastian, brother of Viola
Antonio, a sea captain, friend to Viola
A Sea Captain, friend to Viola
Valentine ⎫
Curio ⎭   gentlemen attending on the Duke
Sir Toby Belch, uncle to Olivia
Sir Andrew Aguecheek
Malvolio, steward to Olivia
Fabian ⎫
Feste, a clown ⎭   servants to Olivia
Olivia, a countess
Viola, sister to Sebastian
Maria, Olivia's woman
Lords, a Priest, Sailors, Officers, Musicians, and
  Attendants

Scene: Illyria]

Twelfth Night,
or, What You Will

ACT I

Scene I. [*The Duke's palace.*]

*Enter Orsino, Duke of Illyria, Curio, and other Lords,
[with Musicians].*

Duke. If music be the food of love, play on,
    Give me excess of it, that, surfeiting,
    The appetite°¹ may sicken, and so die.
    That strain again! It had a dying fall;°
    O, it came o'er my ear like the sweet sound   5
    That breathes upon a bank of violets,
    Stealing and giving odor. Enough, no more!
    'Tis not so sweet now as it was before.
    O spirit of love, how quick and fresh° art thou,
    That,° notwithstanding thy capacity,   10
    Receiveth as the sea. Nought enters there,°
    Of what validity and pitch° soe'er,
    But falls into abatement and low price°

---

¹ The degree sign (°) indicates a footnote, which is keyed to the
text by line number. Text references are printed in **boldface** type;
the annotation follows in roman type.
I.i.3 **appetite** i.e., the lover's appetite for music   4 **fall** cadence
9 **quick and fresh** lively and eager   10 **That** in that   11 **there** i.e.,
in the lover's "capacity"   12 **validity and pitch** value and superiority
(in falconry, pitch is the highest point of a bird's flight)   13 **price**
esteem

       Even in a minute. So full of shapes° is fancy°
15   That it alone is high fantastical.°

Curio. Will you go hunt, my lord?

Duke. What, Curio?

Curio. The hart.

Duke. Why, so I do, the noblest that I have.
20   O, when mine eyes did see Olivia first,
       Methought she purged the air of pestilence.
       That instant was I turned into a hart,
       And my desires, like fell° and cruel hounds,
       E'er since pursue me.°

                Enter Valentine.

                              How now? What news from her?

25 *Valentine.* So please my lord, I might not be admitted;
       But from her handmaid do return this answer:
       The element° itself, till seven years' heat,°
       Shall not behold her face at ample view;
       But like a cloistress she will veilèd walk,
30   And water once a day her chamber round
       With eye-offending brine: all this to season°
       A brother's dead love, which she would keep fresh
       And lasting in her sad remembrance.°

Duke. O, she that hath a heart of that fine frame
35   To pay this debt of love but to a brother,
       How will she love when the rich golden shaft°
       Hath killed the flock of all affections else°

14 **shapes** fantasies   14 **fancy** love   15 **high fantastical** preeminently
imaginative   23 **fell** fierce   22–24 **That instant . . . pursue me** (Orsino's mannered play on "hart-heart"—which exemplifies the lover's
"high fantastical" wit—derives from the story of Actaeon, a famous
hunter who, having seen Diana bathing, was transformed into a stag
and torn to pieces by his hounds)   27 **element** sky   27 **heat** course
31 **season** preserve (by the salt in her tears)   33 **remembrance** (pronounced with four syllables, "re-mem-ber-ance")   36 **golden shaft**
(the shaft, borne by Cupid, that causes love, as distinguished from the
leaden shaft, which causes aversion and disdain)   37 **all affections
else** i.e., all other emotions but love

That live in her; when liver, brain, and heart,°
These sovereign thrones, are all supplied and filled,
Her sweet perfections,° with one self° king.   *40*
Away before me to sweet beds of flow'rs;
Love-thoughts lie rich when canopied with bow'rs.

                                        Exeunt.

Scene II. [*The seacoast.*]

Enter Viola, a Captain, and Sailors.

Viola. What country, friends, is this?

Captain. This is Illyria,° lady.

Viola. And what should I do in Illyria?
My brother he is in Elysium.°
Perchance he is not drowned. What think you, sailors?   *5*

Captain. It is perchance that you yourself were saved.

Viola. O my poor brother, and so perchance may he be.

Captain. True, madam; and, to comfort you with
    chance,°
Assure yourself, after our ship did split,
When you, and those poor number saved with you,   *10*
Hung on our driving° boat, I saw your brother,
Most provident in peril, bind himself
(Courage and hope both teaching him the practice)°
To a strong mast that lived° upon the sea;
Where, like Arion° on the dolphin's back,   *15*

38 **liver, brain, and heart** (the seats respectively of sexual desire,
thought, and feeling)   40 **perfections** (pronounced with four syllables)   40 **self** sole   I.ii.2 **Illyria** region bordering the east coast of
the Adriatic   4 **Elysium** heaven (in classical mythology, the abode
of the happy dead)   8 **chance** possibility   11 **driving** drifting   13
practice procedure   14 **lived** i.e., floated   15 **Arion** (in classical
mythology, a bard who, having leapt into the sea to escape from
murderous sailors, was borne to shore by a dolphin that he charmed
by his songs)

I saw him hold acquaintance with the waves
So long as I could see.

Viola. For saying so, there's gold.
Mine own escape unfoldeth to my hope,°
Whereto thy speech serves for authority°
The like of him. Know'st thou this country?

Captain. Ay, madam, well, for I was bred and born
Not three hours' travel from this very place.

Viola. Who governs here?

Captain. A noble duke, in nature as in name.

Viola. What is his name?

Captain. Orsino.

Viola. Orsino! I have heard my father name him.
He was a bachelor then.

Captain. And so is now, or was so very late;
For but a month ago I went from hence,
And then 'twas fresh in murmur° (as you know
What great ones do, the less will prattle of)
That he did seek the love of fair Olivia.

Viola. What's she?

Captain. A virtuous maid, the daughter of a count
That died some twelvemonth since, then leaving her
In the protection of his son, her brother,
Who shortly also died; for whose dear love,
They say, she hath abjured the sight
And company of men.

Viola.   O that I served that lady,
And might not be delivered° to the world,
Till I had made mine own occasion mellow,
What my estate is.°

Captain.   That were hard to compass,°

19 **unfoldeth to my hope** i.e., reinforces my hope for my brother's
safety   20 **serves for authority** i.e., tends to justify   32 **fresh in
murmur** i.e., being rumored   42 **delivered** disclosed   43–44 **made
mine . . . estate is** found an appropriate time to reveal my status
44 **compass** effect

Because she will admit no kind of suit,   45
No, not° the Duke's.

Viola. There is a fair behavior in thee, captain,
And though that° nature with a beauteous wall
Doth oft close in° pollution, yet of thee
I will believe thou hast a mind that suits   50
With this thy fair and outward character.°
I prithee (and I'll pay thee bounteously)
Conceal me what I am, and be my aid
For such disguise as haply shall become
The form of my intent.° I'll serve this duke.   55
Thou shalt present me as an eunuch to him;
It may be worth thy pains. For I can sing,
And speak to him in many sorts of music
That will allow° me very worth his service.
What else may hap, to time I will commit;   60
Only shape thou thy silence to my wit.°

Captain. Be you his eunuch,° and your mute I'll be;
When my tongue blabs, then let mine eyes not see.

Viola. I thank thee. Lead me on.   *Exeunt.*

Scene III. [*Olivia's house.*]

Enter Sir Toby and Maria.

Toby. What a plague means my niece to take the death
of her brother thus? I am sure care's an enemy to
life.

Maria. By my troth, Sir Toby, you must come in

---

46 **not** not even   48 **though that** even though   49 **close in** conceal
51 **character** i.e., appearance and demeanor   54–55 **become/The
form of my intent** i.e., suit my purpose   59 **allow** certify   61 **wit**
i.e., skill in carrying out my plan   62 **Be you his eunuch** (this part of
the plan was not carried out)

5   earlier a' nights. Your cousin,° my lady, takes great
      exceptions to your ill hours.

Toby. Why, let her except before excepted.°

Maria. Ay, but you must confine yourself within the
      modest limits of order.°

10 *Toby.* Confine? I'll confine° myself no finer than I am.
      These clothes are good enough to drink in, and so
      be these boots too. And° they be not, let them hang
      themselves in their own straps.

Maria. That quaffing and drinking will undo you. I
15   heard my lady talk of it yesterday; and of a foolish
      knight that you brought in one night here to be her
      wooer.

Toby. Who? Sir Andrew Aguecheek?

Maria. Ay, he.

20 *Toby.* He's as tall° a man as any's in Illyria.

Maria. What's that to th' purpose?

Toby. Why, he has three thousand ducats a year.

Maria. Ay, but he'll have but a year in all these ducats.
      He's a very fool and a prodigal.

25 *Toby.* Fie that you'll say so! He plays o' th' viol-de-
      gamboys,° and speaks three or four languages word
      for word without book, and hath all the good gifts
      of nature.

Maria. He hath indeed all, most natural;° for, besides
30   that he's a fool, he's a great quarreler; and but that
      he hath the gift of a coward to allay the gust° he
      hath in quarreling, 'tis thought among the prudent
      he would quickly have the gift of a grave.

I.iii.5 **cousin** (a term indicating various degrees of kinship; here,
niece)   7 **except before excepted** (Sir Toby parodies the legal jargon
exceptis exceptiendis ["with the exceptions previously noted"] commonly used in leases and contracts)   9 **modest limits of order** reasonable limits of good behavior   10 **confine** i.e., clothe   12 **And** if (a
common Elizabethan usage)   20 **tall** i.e., bold and handsome   25–
26 **viol-de-gamboys** bass viol   29 **natural** i.e., like a natural fool or
idiot   31 **gust** gusto

Toby. By this hand, they are scoundrels and sub-
stractors° that say so of him. Who are they?   *35*

Maria. They that add, moreover, he's drunk nightly in
your company.

Toby. With drinking healths to my niece. I'll drink to
her as long as there is a passage in my throat and
drink in Illyria. He's a coward and a coistrel° that   *40*
will not drink to my niece till his brains turn o' th'
toe like a parish top.° What, wench? *Castiliano
vulgo;*° for here comes Sir Andrew Agueface.

Enter Sir Andrew.

Andrew. Sir Toby Belch. How now, Sir Toby Belch?

Toby. Sweet Sir Andrew.   *45*

Andrew. Bless you, fair shrew.

Maria. And you too, sir.

Toby. Accost, Sir Andrew, accost.

Andrew. What's that?

Toby. My niece's chambermaid.°   *50*

Andrew. Good Mistress Accost, I desire better acquaintance.

Maria. My name is Mary, sir.

Andrew. Good Mistress Mary Accost.

34–35 **substractors** slanderers   40 **coistrel** knave (literally, a groom
who takes care of a knight's horse)   42 **parish top** (according to
George Steevens, a large top "formerly kept in every village, to be
whipped in frosty weather, that the peasants might be kept warm
by exercise, and out of mischief while they could not work"; however, the allusion may be to the communal top-spinning whose
origins are buried in religious ritual)   42–43 **Castiliano vulgo** (a
phrase of uncertain meaning; perhaps Sir Toby is suggesting that
Maria assume a grave and ceremonial manner—like that of the
notoriously formal Castilians—for Sir Andrew's benefit)   49–50
What's that?/My niece's chambermaid (Sir Andrew asks the meaning of the word "accost," but Sir Toby thinks that he is referring to
Maria. Actually, she was not Olivia's chambermaid, but rather her
companion, or lady in waiting, as is made clear at I.v.162)

55 *Toby.* You mistake, knight. "Accost" is front her, board her, woo her, assail her.

Andrew. By my troth, I would not undertake her in this company. Is that the meaning of "accost"?

Maria. Fare you well, gentlemen.

60 *Toby.* And thou let part so,° Sir Andrew, would thou mightst never draw sword again.

Andrew. And you part so, mistress, I would I might never draw sword again! Fair lady, do you think you have fools in hand?°

65 *Maria.* Sir, I have not you by th' hand.

Andrew. Marry,° but you shall have, and here's my hand.

Maria. Now, sir, thought is free. I pray you, bring your hand to th' butt'ry° bar and let it drink.

70 *Andrew.* Wherefore, sweetheart? What's your metaphor?

Maria. It's dry,° sir.

Andrew. Why, I think so. I am not such an ass but I can keep my hand dry. But what's your jest?

75 *Maria.* A dry jest, sir.

Andrew. Are you full of them?

Maria. Ay, sir, I have them at my finger's ends. Marry, now I let go your hand, I am barren.° *Exit Maria.*

Toby. O knight, thou lack'st a cup of canary!° When
80 did I see thee so put down?

Andrew. Never in your life, I think, unless you see canary put me down. Methinks sometimes I have

60 **so** i.e., without ceremony   64 **have fools in hand** i.e., are dealing with fools   66 **Marry** indeed (a mild interjection, originally an oath by the Virgin Mary)   69 **butt'ry** buttery, a storeroom for butts or casks of liquor   72 **dry** (1) thirsty (2) indicative of impotence   78 **barren** (1) without more jests (2) dull-witted   79 **canary** a sweet wine from the Canary Islands

no more wit than a Christian or an ordinary man
has. But I am a great eater of beef, and I believe
that does harm to my wit.   85

Toby. No question.

Andrew. And I thought that, I'd forswear it. I'll ride
home tomorrow, Sir Toby.

Toby. Pourquoi,° my dear knight?

Andrew. What is "*pourquoi*"? Do, or not do? I would   90
I had bestowed that time in the tongues that I have
in fencing, dancing, and bearbaiting. O, had I but
followed the arts!

Toby. Then hadst thou had an excellent head of hair.°

Andrew. Why, would that have mended my hair?   95

Toby. Past question, for thou seest it will not curl by
nature.

Andrew. But it becomes me well enough, does't not?

Toby. Excellent. It hangs like flax on a distaff;° and
I hope to see a huswife° take thee between her legs   100
and spin it off.

Andrew. Faith, I'll home tomorrow, Sir Toby. Your
niece will not be seen; or if she be, it's four to one
she'll none of me. The Count himself here hard by
woos her.   105

Toby. She'll none o' th' Count. She'll not match above
her degree, neither in estate,° years, nor wit; I have
heard her swear't. Tut, there's life in't,° man.

Andrew. I'll stay a month longer. I am a fellow o' th'
strangest mind i' th' world. I delight in masques and 110
revels sometimes altogether.

Toby. Art thou good at these kickshawses,° knight?

89 **Pourquoi** why (French)   94 **Then hadst thou had an excellent
head of hair** (perhaps Sir Toby is punning on Sir Andrew's "tongues"
[line 91] as "tongs" or curling irons)   99 **distaff** stick used in spin-
ning   100 **huswife** housewife   107 **estate** fortune   108 **there's life
in't** i.e., there's hope for you yet   112 **kickshawses** trifles (French
quelque chose)

Andrew. As any man in Illyria, whatsoever he be, under the degree of my betters,° and yet I will not
115　compare with an old° man.

Toby. What is thy excellence in a galliard,° knight?

Andrew. Faith, I can cut a caper.°

Toby. And I can cut the mutton to't.

Andrew. And I think I have the back-trick° simply as
120　strong as any man in Illyria.

Toby. Wherefore are these things hid? Wherefore have these gifts a curtain before 'em? Are they like to take° dust, like Mistress Mall's picture? Why dost thou not go to church in a galliard and come home
125　in a coranto?° My very walk should be a jig. I would not so much as make water but in a sink-a-pace.° What dost thou mean? Is it a world to hide virtues° in? I did think, by the excellent constitution of thy leg, it was formed under the star of a
130　galliard.°

Andrew. Ay, 'tis strong, and it does indifferent well in a damned-colored stock.° Shall we set about some revels?

Toby. What shall we do else? Were we not born under
135　Taurus?°

Andrew. Taurus? That's sides and heart.

114 **under the degree of my betters** i.e., so long as he is not my social superior　115 **old** i.e., experienced (?)　116 **galliard** lively dance in triple time　117 **caper** (1) frisky leap (2) spice used to season mutton (hence Sir Toby's remark in the next line)　119 **back-trick** reverse step in dancing　123 **take** gather　125 **coranto** quick running dance　126–27 **sink-a-pace** cinquepace (French *cinque pas*), a kind of galliard of five steps (but there is also a scatological pun here)　128 **virtues** talents, accomplishments　129–30 **the star of a galliard** i.e., a dancing star　132 **damned-colored stock** (of the many emendations proposed for this stocking of uncertain color—"damasked-colored," "dun-colored," "dove-colored," "damson-colored," and the like—Rowe's "flame-colored" has been most popular)　135 **Taurus** the Bull (one of the twelve signs of the zodiac, each of which was thought to influence a certain part of the human body. Most authorities assigned Taurus to neither "sides and heart" nor "legs and thighs," but to neck and throat)

Toby. No, sir; it is legs and thighs. Let me see thee
caper. Ha, higher; ha, ha, excellent!   *Exeunt.*

Scene IV. [*The Duke's palace.*]

Enter Valentine, and Viola in man's attire.

Valentine. If the Duke continue these favors towards
you, Cesario, you are like to be much advanced.
He hath known you but three days and already you
are no stranger.

Viola. You either fear his humor° or my negligence,   *5*
that° you call in question the continuance of his
love. Is he inconstant, sir, in his favors?

Valentine. No, believe me.

Enter Duke, Curio, and Attendants.

Viola. I thank you. Here comes the Count.

Duke. Who saw Cesario, ho?   *10*

Viola. On your attendance, my lord, here.

Duke. Stand you awhile aloof. Cesario,
Thou know'st no less but all.° I have unclasped
To thee the book even of my secret soul.
Therefore, good youth, address thy gait° unto her;   *15*
Be not denied access, stand at her doors,
And tell them there thy fixèd foot shall grow
Till thou have audience.

Viola.   Sure, my noble lord,
If she be so abandoned to her sorrow
As it is spoke, she never will admit me.   *20*

I.iv.5 **humor** changeable disposition   6 **that** in that   13 **no less but
all** i.e., everything   15 **address thy gait** direct your steps

Duke. Be clamorous and leap all civil bounds
    Rather than make unprofited° return.

Viola. Say I do speak with her, my lord, what then?

Duke. O, then unfold the passion of my love;
25   Surprise her with discourse of my dear° faith;
    It shall become thee well to act my woes.
    She will attend it better in thy youth
    Than in a nuncio's° of more grave aspect.°

Viola. I think not so, my lord.

Duke.   Dear lad, believe it;
30   For they shall yet belie thy happy years
    That say thou art a man. Diana's lip
    Is not more smooth and rubious;° thy small pipe°
    Is as the maiden's organ, shrill and sound,°
    And all is semblative° a woman's part.
35   I know thy constellation° is right apt°
    For this affair. Some four or five attend him,
    All, if you will; for I myself am best
    When least in company. Prosper well in this,
    And thou shalt live as freely as thy lord
    To call his fortunes thine.

40 *Viola.*   I'll do my best
    To woo your lady. [*Aside*] Yet a barful° strife!
    Whoe'er I woo, myself would be his wife.   *Exeunt.*

---

22 **unprofited** unsuccessful   25 **dear** intense   28 **nuncio's** messenger's   28 **aspect** (accent on second syllable)   32 **rubious** ruby-red   32 **pipe** voice   33 **shrill and sound** high and clear   34 **semblative** like   35 **constellation** predetermined qualities   35 **apt** suitable   41 **barful** full of impediments

Scene V. [*Olivia's house.*]

Enter Maria and Clown.

Maria. Nay, either tell me where thou hast been, or I
will not open my lips so wide as a bristle may enter
in way of thy excuse. My lady will hang thee for
thy absence.

Clown. Let her hang me. He that is well hanged in   5
this world needs to fear no colors.°

Maria. Make that good.°

Clown. He shall see none to fear.

Maria. A good lenten° answer. I can tell thee where
that saying was born, of "I fear no colors."   10

Clown. Where, good Mistress Mary?

Maria. In the wars; and that may you be bold to say
in your foolery.

Clown. Well, God give them wisdom that have it, and
those that are fools, let them use their talents.°   15

Maria. Yet you will be hanged for being so long ab-
sent, or to be turned away. Is not that as good as a
hanging to you?

Clown. Many a good hanging prevents a bad marriage,
and for turning away, let summer bear it out.°   20

I.v.6 **fear no colors** i.e., fear nothing (with a pun on "color" meaning
"flag" and "collar" meaning "hangman's noose")   7 **Make that
good** i.e., explain it   9 **lenten** thin, meager (perhaps an allusion to
the colorless, unbleached linen that replaced the customary liturgical
purple or violet during Lent)   15 **talents** native intelligence (with
perhaps a pun on "talons" meaning "claws")   20 **let summer bear
it out** i.e., let the warm weather make it endurable

Maria. You are resolute then?

Clown. Not so, neither; but I am resolved on two
   points.°

Maria. That if one break, the other will hold; or if
25   both break, your gaskins° fall.

Clown. Apt, in good faith; very apt. Well, go thy way!
   If Sir Toby would leave drinking, thou wert as
   witty a piece of Eve's flesh° as any in Illyria.

Maria. Peace, you rogue; no more o' that. Here comes
30   my lady. Make your excuse wisely, you were best.°
                                                   [*Exit.*]

*Enter Lady Olivia with Malvolio
[and other Attendants].*

Clown. Wit, and't° be thy will, put me into good
   fooling. Those wits that think they have thee do
   very oft prove fools, and I that am sure I lack thee
   may pass for a wise man. For what says Quina-
35   palus?° "Better a witty fool than a foolish wit."
   God bless thee, lady.

Olivia. Take the fool away.

Clown. Do you not hear, fellows? Take away the lady.

Olivia. Go to,° y' are a dry° fool! I'll no more of you.
40   Besides, you grow dishonest.°

Clown. Two faults, madonna,° that drink and good
   counsel will amend. For give the dry° fool drink,
   then is the fool not dry. Bid the dishonest man
   mend himself: if he mend, he is no longer dishonest;
45   if he cannot, let the botcher° mend him. Anything

23 **points** counts (but Maria takes it in the sense of tagged laces
serving as suspenders)   25 **gaskins** loose breeches   27–28 **thou wert
as witty a piece of Eve's flesh** i.e., you would make as clever a wife
30 **you were best** it would be best for you   31 **and't** if it   34–35 **Quin-
apalus** (a sage of the Clown's invention)   39 **Go to** enough   39 **dry**
stupid   40 **dishonest** unreliable   41 **madonna** my lady   42 **dry**
thirsty   45 **botcher** mender of clothes

that's mended is but patched; virtue that trans-
gresses is but patched with sin, and sin that amends
is but patched with virtue. If that this simple syllo-
gism will serve, so; if it will not, what remedy? As
there is no true cuckold but calamity,° so beauty's   *50*
a flower. The lady bade take away the fool; therefore, I say again, take her away.

Olivia. Sir, I bade them take away you.

Clown. Misprision in the highest degree.° Lady, *cucullus non facit monachum.*° That's as much to say   *55*
as, I wear not motley in my brain. Good madonna,
give me leave to prove·you a fool.

Olivia. Can you do it?

Clown. Dexteriously,° good madonna.

Olivia. Make your proof.   *60*

Clown. I must catechize you for it, madonna. Good
my mouse of virtue,° answer me.

Olivia. Well, sir, for want of other idleness,° I'll bide
your proof.

Clown. Good madonna, why mourn'st thou?   *65*

Olivia. Good fool, for my brother's death.

Clown. I think his soul is in hell, madonna.

Olivia. I know his soul is in heaven, fool.

Clown. The more fool, madonna, to mourn for your
brother's soul, being in heaven. Take away the fool,   *70*
gentlemen.

50 **there is no true cuckold but calamity** (although the Clown's chat-
ter should not be pressed too hard for significance, Kittredge's para-
phrase of this difficult passage is perhaps the least unsatisfactory:
"Every man is wedded to fortune; hence, when one's fortune is unfaithful, one may in very truth be called a cuckold—the husband of
an unfaithful wife")   54 **Misprision in the highest degree** i.e., an
egregious error in mistaken identity   54–55 **cucullus non facit
monachum** a cowl does not make a monk   59 **Dexteriously** dexter-
ously   61–62 **Good my mouse of virtue** my good virtuous mouse (a
term of playful affection)   63 **idleness** trifling

Olivia. What think you of this fool, Malvolio? Doth
he not mend?

Malvolio. Yes, and shall do till the pangs of death
75   shake him. Infirmity, that decays the wise, doth
ever make the better fool.

Clown. God send you, sir, a speedy infirmity, for the
better increasing your folly. Sir Toby will be sworn
that I am no fox,° but he will not pass his word for
80   twopence that you are no fool.

Olivia. How say you to that, Malvolio?

Malvolio. I marvel your ladyship takes delight in such
a barren° rascal. I saw him put down the other day
with° an ordinary fool that has no more brain than
85   a stone. Look you now, he's out of his guard°
already. Unless you laugh and minister occasion°
to him, he is gagged. I protest I take these wise men
that crow° so at these set° kind of fools no better
than the fools' zanies.°

90   *Olivia.* O, you are sick of self-love, Malvolio, and
taste with a distempered appetite. To be generous,°
guiltless, and of free disposition, is to take those
things for birdbolts° that you deem cannon bullets.
There is no slander in an allowed° fool, though
95   he do nothing but rail; nor no railing in a known
discreet man, though he do nothing but reprove.

Clown. Now Mercury indue thee with leasing,° for
thou speak'st well of fools.

Enter Maria.

Maria. Madam, there is at the gate a young gentleman
100   much desires to speak with you.

79 **I am no fox** i.e., sly and dangerous (like you)   83 **barren** stupid
83–84 **put down ... with** bested ... by   85 **out of his guard** defense-
less   86 **minister occasion** afford opportunity (for his fooling)
88 **crow** i.e., with laughter   88 **set** artificial   89 **zanies** inferior buf-
foons   91 **generous** liberal-minded   93 **birdbolts** blunt arrows   94
allowed licensed, privileged   97 **Mercury indue thee with leasing**
may the god of trickery endow you with the gift of deception

Olivia. From the Count Orsino, is it?

Maria. I know not, madam. 'Tis a fair young man,
and well attended.

Olivia. Who of my people hold him in delay?

Maria. Sir Toby, madam, your kinsman. *105*

Olivia. Fetch him off, I pray you. He speaks nothing
but madman. Fie on him! [*Exit Maria.*] Go you,
Malvolio. If it be a suit from the Count, I am sick,
or not at home. What you will, to dismiss it. (*Exit
Malvolio.*) Now you see, sir, how your fooling *110*
grows old,° and people dislike it.

Clown. Thou hast spoke for us, madonna, as if thy
eldest son should be a fool; whose skull Jove°
cram with brains, for—here he comes—one of thy
kin has a most weak pia mater.° *115*

Enter Sir Toby.

Olivia. By mine honor, half drunk. What is he at the
gate, cousin?

Toby. A gentleman.

Olivia. A gentleman? What gentleman?

Toby. 'Tis a gentleman here. A plague o' these pickle- *120*
herring!° How now, sot?°

Clown. Good Sir Toby.

Olivia. Cousin,° cousin, how have you come so early
by this lethargy?

Toby. Lechery? I defy lechery. There's one at the gate. *125*

Olivia. Ay, marry, what is he?

---

111 **old** stale, tedious   113 **Jove** (if, as is likely, Shakespeare here
and elsewhere wrote "God," the printed text reflects the statute of
1606 that prohibited profane stage allusions to the deity)   115 **pia
mater** brain   120–21 **pickle-herring** (to which the drunken Sir Toby
attributes his hiccoughing)   121 **sot** fool   123 **Cousin** i.e., uncle
(see I.iii.5)

Toby. Let him be the devil and he will, I care not. Give me faith,° say I. Well, it's all one.   *Exit.*

Olivia. What's a drunken man like, fool?

130 *Clown.* Like a drowned man, a fool, and a madman. One draught above heat° makes him a fool, the second mads him, and a third drowns him.

Olivia. Go thou and seek the crowner,° and let him sit o' my coz;° for he's in the third degree of drink—
135 he's drowned. Go look after him.

Clown. He is but mad yet, madonna, and the fool shall look to the madman.   [*Exit.*]

Enter Malvolio.

Malvolio. Madam, yond young fellow swears he will speak with you. I told him you were sick; he takes
140 on him to understand so much, and therefore comes to speak with you. I told him you were asleep; he seems to have a foreknowledge of that too, and therefore comes to speak with you. What is to be said to him, lady? He's fortified against any denial.

145 *Olivia.* Tell him he shall not speak with me.

Malvolio. H'as° been told so; and he says he'll stand at your door like a sheriff's post,° and be the supporter to a bench, but° he'll speak with you.

Olivia. What kind o' man is he?

150 *Malvolio.* Why, of mankind.°

Olivia. What manner of man?

Malvolio. Of very ill manner. He'll speak with you, will you or no.

---

128 **faith** (in order to resist the devil)   131 **above heat** i.e., above what is required to make a man normally warm   133 **crowner** coroner   134 **sit o' my coz** hold an inquest on my kinsman   146 **H'as** he has   147 **sheriff's post** post set up before a sheriff's door for placards, notices, and such   148 **but** except   150 **of mankind** i.e., like other men

Olivia. Of what personage and years is he?

Malvolio. Not yet old enough for a man nor young 155
enough for a boy; as a squash° is before 'tis a
peascod, or a codling° when 'tis almost an apple.
'Tis with him in standing water,° between boy and
man. He is very well-favored and he speaks very
shrewishly.° One would think his mother's milk 160
were scarce out of him.

Olivia. Let him approach. Call in my gentlewoman.

Malvolio. Gentlewoman, my lady calls.   *Exit.*

Enter Maria.

Olivia. Give me my veil; come, throw it o'er my face.
We'll once more hear Orsino's embassy.   165

Enter Viola.

Viola. The honorable lady of the house, which is she?

Olivia. Speak to me; I shall answer for her. Your will?

Viola. Most radiant, exquisite, and unmatchable beauty
—I pray you tell me if this be the lady of the house,
for I never saw her. I would be loath to cast away 170
my speech; for, besides that it is excellently well
penned, I have taken great pains to con° it. Good
beauties, let me sustain no scorn. I am very comptible,° even to the least sinister° usage.

Olivia. Whence came you, sir?   175

Viola. I can say little more than I have studied, and
that question's out of my part. Good gentle one,
give me modest° assurance if you be the lady of the
house, that I may proceed in my speech.

156 **squash** unripe peascod (pea pod)   157 **codling** unripe apple
158 **standing water** i.e., at the turning of the tide, between ebb and
flood, when it flows neither way   160 **shrewishly** tartly   172 **con**
learn   173–74 **comptible** sensitive   174 **sinister** discourteous   178
modest reasonable

180 *Olivia.* Are you a comedian?°

Viola. No, my profound heart;° and yet (by the very
fangs of malice I swear) I am not that° I play.
Are you the lady of the house?

Olivia. If I do not usurp° myself, I am.

185 *Viola.* Most certain, if you are she, you do usurp
yourself; for what° is yours to bestow is not yours
to reserve. But this is from my commission.° I will
on with my speech in your praise and then show
you the heart of my message.

190 *Olivia.* Come to what is important in't. I forgive you°
the praise.

Viola. Alas, I took great pains to study it, and 'tis
poetical.

Olivia. It is the more like to be feigned; I pray you
195 keep it in. I heard you were saucy at my gates; and
allowed your approach rather to wonder at you
than to hear you. If you be not mad, be gone; if
you have reason, be brief. 'Tis not that time of
moon with me to make one in so skipping a dia-
200 logue.°

Maria. Will you hoist sail, sir? Here lies your way.

Viola. No, good swabber; I am to hull° here a little
longer. Some mollification for your giant,° sweet
lady. Tell me your mind. I am a messenger.°

205 *Olivia.* Sure you have some hideous matter to deliver,
when the courtesy of it is so fearful.° Speak your
office.°

180 **comedian** actor (because he has had to "con" a "part")   181 **my
profound heart** my sagacious lady (a bantering compliment)
182 **that** that which   184 **usurp** counterfeit (but Viola takes it in the
sense "betray," "wrong")   186 **what** i.e., your hand in marriage
187 **from my commission** beyond my instructions   190 **forgive you**
excuse you from repeating   198–200 **'Tis not ... dialogue** i.e., I am
not in the mood to sustain such aimless banter   202 **hull** lie adrift
203 **giant** (an ironical reference to Maria's small size)   204 **Tell me
your mind. I am a messenger.** (Many editors have divided these
sentences, assigning the first to Olivia and the second to Viola)
206 **when the courtesy of it is so fearful** i.e., since your manner is so
truculent   207 **office** business

Viola. It alone concerns your ear. I bring no overture
of war, no taxation of° homage. I hold the olive°
in my hand. My words are as full of peace as   210
matter.°

Olivia. Yet you began rudely. What are you? What
would you?

Viola. The rudeness that hath appeared in me have I
learned from my entertainment.° What I am, and   215
what I would, are as secret as maidenhead:° to
your ears, divinity;° to any other's, profanation.

Olivia. Give us the place alone; we will hear this
divinity. [*Exit Maria and Attendants.*] Now, sir,
what is your text?   220

Viola. Most sweet lady—

Olivia. A comfortable° doctrine, and much may be
said of it. Where lies your text?

Viola. In Orsino's bosom.

Olivia. In his bosom? In what chapter of his bosom?   225

Viola. To answer by the method,° in the first of his
heart.

Olivia. O, I have read it; it is heresy. Have you no
more to say?

Viola. Good madam, let me see your face.   230

Olivia. Have you any commission from your lord to
negotiate with my face? You are now out of your
text.° But we will draw the curtain and show you
the picture. [*Unveils.*] Look you, sir, such a one I
was this present.° Is't not well done?   235

209 **taxation of** demand for   209 **olive** (the symbol of peace)
211 **matter** significant content   215 **entertainment** reception   216
maidenhead maidenhood   217 **divinity** i.e., a sacred message
222 **comfortable** comforting   226 **method** i.e., in the theological
style suggested by "divinity," "profanation," "text," and "doctrine"
232–33 **You are now out of your text** i.e., you have shifted from
talking of your master's heart to asking about my face   235 **this
present** just now (like portrait painters, Olivia gives the age of the
subject of the "picture" she has just revealed by drawing the "curtain" of a veil from her face)

Viola. Excellently done, if God did all.

Olivia. 'Tis in grain,° sir; 'twill endure wind and
weather.

Viola. 'Tis beauty truly blent, whose red and white
240   Nature's own sweet and cunning° hand laid on.
Lady, you are the cruel'st she alive
If you will lead these graces to the grave,
And leave the world no copy.

Olivia. O, sir, I will not be so hard-hearted. I will give
245   out divers schedules° of my beauty. It shall be in-
ventoried, and every particle and utensil° labeled
to my will:° as, item,° two lips, indifferent red;
item, two gray eyes, with lids to them; item, one
neck, one chin, and so forth. Were you sent hither
250   to praise° me?

Viola. I see you what you are; you are too proud;
But if° you were the devil, you are fair.
My lord and master loves you. O, such love
Could be but recompensed though you were crowned
The nonpareil of beauty.

255 *Olivia.*   How does he love me?

Viola. With adorations, with fertile° tears,
With groans that thunder love, with sighs of fire.

Olivia. Your lord does know my mind; I cannot love
him.
Yet I suppose him virtuous, know him noble,
260   Of great estate, of fresh and stainless youth;
In voices well divulged,° free, learned, and valiant,
And in dimension° and the shape of nature
A gracious person. But yet I cannot love him.
He might have took his answer long ago.

265 *Viola.* If I did love you in my master's flame,

237 **in grain** fast-dyed, indelible 240 **cunning** skillful 245 **sched-**
ules statements 246 **utensil** article 246–47 **labeled to my will** i.e.,
added as a codicil 247 **item** also 250 **praise** appraise 252 **if** even
if 256 **fertile** copious 261 **well divulged** i.e., of good repute
262 **dimension** physique

With such a suff'ring, such a deadly° life,
In your denial I would find no sense;
I would not understand it.

Olivia.   Why, what would you?

Viola. Make me a willow° cabin at your gate
And call upon my soul° within the house;   270
Write loyal cantons° of contemnèd° love
And sing them loud even in the dead of night;
Hallo your name to the reverberate° hills
And make the babbling gossip of the air°
Cry out "Olivia!" O, you should not rest   275
Between the elements of air and earth
But° you should pity me.

Olivia. You might do much. What is your parentage?

Viola. Above my fortunes, yet my state° is well.
I am a gentleman.

Olivia.   Get you to your lord.   280
I cannot love him. Let him send no more,
Unless, perchance, you come to me again
To tell me how he takes it. Fare you well.
I thank you for your pains. Spend this for me.

Viola. I am no fee'd post,° lady; keep your purse;   285
My master, not myself, lacks recompense.
Love make his heart of flint that you shall love;°
And let your fervor, like my master's, be
Placed in contempt. Farewell, fair cruelty.   *Exit.*

Olivia. "What is your parentage?"   290
"Above my fortunes, yet my state is well.
I am a gentleman." I'll be sworn thou art.
Thy tongue, thy face, thy limbs, actions, and spirit

---

266 **deadly** doomed to die   269 **willow** (emblem of a disconsolate
lover)   270 **my soul** i.e., Olivia   271 **cantons** songs   271 **con-
temnèd** rejected   273 **reverberate** reverberating   274 **babbling gossip of the air** i.e., echo   277 **But** but that   279 **state** status   285 **fee'd
post** i.e., lackey to be tipped   287 **Love make ... love** may Love
make the heart of him you love like flint

Do give thee fivefold blazon.° Not too fast; soft,°
        soft,
295 Unless the master were the man. How now?
Even so quickly may one catch the plague?
Methinks I feel this youth's perfections
With an invisible and subtle stealth
To creep in at mine eyes. Well, let it be.
What ho, Malvolio!

Enter Malvolio.

300 *Malvolio.*   Here, madam, at your service.

Olivia. Run after that same peevish° messenger,
The County's° man. He left this ring behind him,
Would I or not. Tell him I'll none of it.
Desire him not to flatter with° his lord
305 Nor hold him up with hopes. I am not for him.
If that the youth will come this way tomorrow,
I'll give him reasons for't. Hie thee, Malvolio.

Malvolio. Madam, I will.   *Exit.*

Olivia. I do I know not what, and fear to find
310 Mine eye too great a flatterer for my mind.°
Fate, show thy force; ourselves we do not owe.°
What is decreed must be—and be this so!   [*Exit.*]

294 **blazon** heraldic insignia   294 **soft** i.e., take it slowly   301 **peev-ish** truculent impertinent   302 **County's** Count's   304 **flatter with** encourage   310 **Mine eye . . . mind** i.e., my eye, so susceptible to external attractions, will betray my judgment   311 **owe** own

ACT II

Scene I. [*The seacoast.*]

Enter Antonio and Sebastian.

Antonio. Will you stay no longer? Nor will you not
that I go with you?

Sebastian. By your patience,° no. My stars shine darkly
over me; the malignancy of my fate might perhaps
distemper° yours. Therefore I shall crave of you   5
your leave, that I may bear my evils alone. It were
a bad recompense for your love to lay any of them
on you.

Antonio. Let me yet know of you whither you are
bound.   10

Sebastian. No, sooth,° sir. My determinate° voyage is
mere extravagancy.° But I perceive in you so excellent a touch of modesty that you will not extort
from me what I am willing to keep in; therefore it
charges me in manners the rather to express myself.°   15
You must know of me then, Antonio, my name is
Sebastian, which I called Roderigo. My father was
that Sebastian of Messaline whom I know you have
heard of. He left behind him myself and a sister,
both born in an hour.° If the heavens had been   20

II.i.3 **patience** permission   5 **distemper** disorder   11 **sooth** truly
11 **determinate** intended   12 **extravagancy** wandering   14–15 **it
charges me . . . myself** i.e., civility requires that I give some account
of myself   20 **in an hour** in the same hour

59

pleased, would we had so ended! But you, sir,
altered that, for some hour before you took me
from the breach° of the sea was my sister drowned.

Antonio. Alas the day!

25 *Sebastian.* A lady, sir, though it was said she much
resembled me, was yet of many accounted beautiful.
But though I could not with such estimable wonder°
overfar believe that, yet thus far I will boldly
publish° her: she bore a mind that envy could not
30 but call fair. She is drowned already, sir, with salt
water, though I seem to drown her remembrance
again with more.

Antonio. Pardon me, sir, your bad entertainment.°

Sebastian. O good Antonio, forgive me your trouble.°

35 *Antonio.* If you will not murder me° for my love, let
me be your servant.

Sebastian. If you will not undo what you have done,
that is, kill him whom you have recovered,° desire
it not. Fare ye well at once. My bosom is full of
40 kindness, and I am yet so near the manners of my
mother that, upon the least occasion more, mine
eyes will tell tales of me.° I am bound to the Count
Orsino's court. Farewell.   *Exit.*

Antonio. The gentleness of all the gods go with thee.
45 I have many enemies in Orsino's court,
Else would I very shortly see thee there.
But come what may, I do adore thee so
That danger shall seem sport, and I will go.   *Exit.*

---

23 **breach** breakers   27 **with such estimable wonder** i.e., with so
much esteem in my appraisal   29 **publish** describe   33 **bad entertainment** i.e., poor reception at my hands   34 **your trouble** the
trouble I have given you   35 **murder me** i.e., by forcing me to part
from you   38 **recovered** saved   40–42 **so near . . . tales of me** i.e.,
so overwrought by my sorrow that, like a woman, I shall weep

Scene II. [*A street near Olivia's house.*]

Enter Viola and Malvolio at several° doors.

Malvolio. Were not you ev'n now with the Countess
Olivia?

Viola. Even now, sir. On a moderate pace I have since
arrived but hither.

Malvolio. She returns this ring to you, sir. You might   *5*
have saved me my pains, to have taken it away
yourself. She adds, moreover, that you should put
your lord into a desperate assurance° she will none
of him. And one thing more, that you be never so
hardy to come again in his affairs, unless it be to   *10*
report your lord's taking of this. Receive it so.

Viola. She took the ring of me.° I'll none of it.

Malvolio. Come, sir, you peevishly threw it to her,
and her will is, it should be so returned. If it be
worth stooping for, there it lies, in your eye;° if   *15*
not, be it his that finds it.   *Exit.*

Viola. I left no ring with her. What means this lady?
Fortune forbid my outside have not charmed her.
She made good view of me; indeed, so much
That sure methought° her eyes had lost her tongue,°   *20*
For she did speak in starts distractedly.
She loves me sure; the cunning° of her passion

II.ii.s.d. **several** separate   8 **desperate assurance** hopeless certainty
12 **She took the ring of me** (of the various emendations proposed for
this puzzling line, Malone's "She took no ring of me" is perhaps the
most attractive)   15 **eye** sight   20 **sure methought** ("sure," which
repairs the defective meter of this line, has been adopted from the
Second Folio. Another common emendation is "as methought")
20 **her eyes had lost her tongue** i.e., her fixed gaze made her lose the
power of speech   22 **cunning** craftiness

Invites me in this churlish messenger.
None of my lord's ring? Why, he sent her none.
25 I am the man.° If it be so, as 'tis,
Poor lady, she were better love a dream.
Disguise, I see thou art a wickedness
Wherein the pregnant enemy° does much.
How easy is it for the proper false°
30 In women's waxen hearts to set their forms!
Alas, our frailty is the cause, not we,
For such as we are made of, such we be.
How will this fadge?° My master loves her dearly;
And I (poor monster)° fond° as much on him;
35 And she (mistaken) seems to dote on me.
What will become of this? As I am man,
My state is desperate° for my master's love.
As I am woman (now alas the day!),
What thriftless° sighs shall poor Olivia breathe?
40 O Time, thou must untangle this, not I;
It is too hard a knot for me t' untie.   [*Exit.*]

Scene III. [*A room in Olivia's house.*]

Enter Sir Toby and Sir Andrew.

Toby. Approach, Sir Andrew. Not to be abed after
midnight is to be up betimes; and *"Deliculo surgere,"*° thou know'st.

Andrew. Nay, by my troth, I know not, but I know
5   to be up late is to be up late.

25 **I am the man** i.e., whom she loves   28 **pregnant enemy** crafty
fiend (i.e., Satan)   29 **proper false** i.e., attractive but deceitful suitors
33 **fadge** turn out   34 **monster** (because of her equivocal position as
both man and woman)   34 **fond** dote   37 **desperate** hopeless   39
thriftless unavailing   II.iii.2–3 **Deliculo surgere** i.e., *Diluculo surgere
saluberrimum est,* "it is most healthful to rise early" (a tag from
William Lily's Latin grammar, which was widely used in sixteenth-
century schools)

Toby. A false conclusion; I hate it as an unfilled can.°
To be up after midnight, and to go to bed then,
is early; so that to go to bed after midnight is to go
to bed betimes. Does not our lives consist of the
four elements?°   *10*

Andrew. Faith, so they say; but I think it rather con-
sists of eating and drinking.

Toby. Th' art a scholar! Let us therefore eat and drink.
Marian I say, a stoup° of wine!

Enter Clown.

Andrew. Here comes the fool, i' faith.   *15*

Clown. How now, my hearts? Did you never see the
picture of We Three?°

Toby. Welcome, ass. Now let's have a catch.°

Andrew. By my troth, the fool has an excellent
breast.° I had rather than forty shillings I had such   *20*
a leg,° and so sweet a breath to sing, as the fool
has. In sooth, thou wast in very gracious° fooling
last night, when thou spok'st of Pigrogromitus,° of
the Vapians° passing the equinoctial of Queubus.°
'Twas very good, i' faith. I sent thee sixpence for   *25*
thy leman.° Hadst it?

Clown. I did impeticos thy gratillity,° for Malvolio's
nose is no whipstock. My lady has a white hand,
and the Myrmidons are no bottle-ale houses.°

6 can tankard   9–10 the four elements i.e., air, fire, earth, and water,
which were thought to be the basic ingredients of all things   14 stoup
cup   16–17 the picture of We Three i.e., a picture of two asses, the
spectator making the third   18 catch round, a simple polyphonic
song for several voices   20 breast voice   21 leg i.e., skill in bowing
(?)   22 gracious delightful   23–24 Pigrogromitus, Vapians, Queubus (presumably words invented by the Clown as specimens of his
"gracious fooling" in mock learning)   26 leman sweetheart   27 impeticos thy gratillity (more of the Clown's fooling, which perhaps
means something like "pocket your gratuity")   27–29 Malvolio's
nose . . . bottle-ale houses (probably mere nonsense)

30 *Andrew*. Excellent. Why, this is the best fooling, when all is done. Now a song!

Toby. Come on, there is sixpence for you. Let's have a song.

Andrew. There's a testril° of me too. If one knight
35 give a——°

Clown. Would you have a love song, or a song of good life?°

Toby. A love song, a love song.

Andrew. Ay, ay, I care not for good life.

Clown sings.

40   O mistress mine, where are you roaming?
    O, stay and hear, your true-love's coming,
       That can sing both high and low.
    Trip no further, pretty sweeting;
    Journeys end in lovers meeting,
45   Every wise man's son doth know.

Andrew. Excellent good, i' faith.

Toby. Good, good.

Clown [sings].

    What is love? 'Tis not hereafter;
    Present mirth hath present laughter;
50   What's to come is still° unsure:
    In delay there lies no plenty;
    Then come kiss me, sweet, and twenty,°
      Youth's a stuff will not endure.

---

34 **testril** tester, sixpence   34–35 **If one knight give a——** (some editors have tried to supply what seems to be a missing line here, but it is probable that the Clown breaks in without permitting Sir Andrew to finish his sentence)   36–37 **of good life** i.e., moral, edifying (?) 50 **still** always   52 **Then come kiss me, sweet, and twenty** i.e., so kiss me, my sweet, and then kiss me twenty times again (some editors, taking "twenty" as an intensive, read the line as "so kiss me then, my very sweet one")

Andrew. A mellifluous voice, as I am true knight.

Toby. A contagious breath.°   55

Andrew. Very sweet and contagious, i' faith.

Toby. To hear by the nose, it is dulcet in contagion.°
But shall we make the welkin° dance indeed? Shall
we rouse the night owl in a catch that will draw
three souls out of one weaver?° Shall we do that?   60

Andrew. And you love me, let's do't. I am dog° at a
catch.

Clown. By'r Lady, sir, and some dogs will catch well.

Andrew. Most certain. Let our catch be "Thou knave."

Clown. "Hold thy peace, thou knave,"° knight? I   65
shall be constrained in't to call thee knave, knight.

Andrew. 'Tis not the first time I have constrained one
to call me knave. Begin, fool. It begins, "Hold thy
peace."

Clown. I shall never begin if I hold my peace.   70

Andrew. Good, i' faith! Come, begin.

Catch sung. Enter Maria.

Maria. What a caterwauling do you keep here? If my
lady have not called up her steward Malvolio and
bid him turn you out of doors, never trust me.

Toby. My lady's a Cataian, we are politicians,° Mal-   75

55 **contagious breath** catchy song   57 **to hear by the nose, it is dulcet
in contagion** i.e., if we could hear through the nose, the Clown's
"breath" would be sweet and not malodorous, as "contagious"
breaths usually are   58 **welkin** sky   60 **weaver** (weavers were noted
for their singing)   61 **dog** clever (but in the next line the Clown
puns on **dog** i.e., latch, gripping device)   65 **Hold thy peace, thou
knave** (a line from the round proposed by Sir Andrew)   75 **My
lady's a Cataian, we are politicians** (because Sir Toby and his companions are "politicians" [i.e., tricksters, intriguers] they recognize
Maria's warning of Olivia's anger as the ruse of a "Cataian" [i.e.,
native of Cathay, cheater]; hence "Tilly-vally, lady" [line 78], which
means something like "Fiddlesticks, lady")

volio's a Peg-a-Ramsey,° and [*sings*] "Three merry
men be we."° Am not I consanguineous?° Am I
not of her blood? Tilly-vally, lady. [*Sings*] "There
dwelt a man in Babylon, lady, lady."

80 *Clown.* Beshrew° me, the knight's in admirable fooling.

Andrew. Ay, he does well enough if he be disposed,
and so do I too. He does it with a better grace, but
I do it more natural.°

85 *Toby.* [*Sings*] "O the twelfth day of December."

Maria. For the love o' God, peace!

Enter Malvolio.

Malvolio. My masters, are you mad? Or what are you?
Have you no wit,° manners, nor honesty,° but to
gabble like tinkers at this time of night? Do ye
90 make an alehouse of my lady's house, that ye squeak
out your coziers'° catches without any mitigation
or remorse° of voice? Is there no respect of place,
persons, nor time in you?

Toby. We did keep time, sir, in our catches. Sneck up.°

95 *Malvolio.* Sir Toby, I must be round° with you. My
lady bade me tell you that, though she harbors
you as her kinsman, she's nothing allied to your
disorders. If you can separate yourself and your
misdemeanors, you are welcome to the house. If
100 not, and it would please you to take leave of her,
she is very willing to bid you farewell.

76 **Peg-a-Ramsey** (character in an old song whose name Sir Toby
uses apparently as a term of contempt)   76–77 **Three merry men be
we** (like Sir Toby's other snatches, a fragment of an old song)
77 **consanguineous** related, kin (to Olivia)   80 **Beshrew** curse
84 **natural** (with an unintentional pun on "natural" as a term for fool
or idiot; see I.iii.29)   88 **wit** sense   88 **honesty** decency   91 **coziers'**
cobblers'   91–92 **mitigation or remorse** i.e., lowering   94 **Sneck up**
go hang   95 **round** blunt

Toby. [*Sings*] "Farewell, dear heart since I must needs
　　be gone."°

Maria. Nay, good Sir Toby.

Clown. [*Sings*] "His eyes do show his days are almost
　　done."

Malvolio. Is't even so?　　　　　　　　　　　　*105*

Toby. [*Sings*] "But I will never die."

Clown. [*Sings*] Sir Toby, there you lie.

Malvolio. This is much credit to you.

Toby. [*Sings*] "Shall I bid him go?"

Clown. [*Sings*] "What and if you do?"　　　　*110*

Toby. [*Sings*] "Shall I bid him go, and spare not?"

Clown. [*Sings*] "O, no, no, no, no, you dare not!"

Toby. Out o' tunc, sir? Ye lie.° Art any more than a
　　steward? Dost thou think, because thou art virtuous,
　　there shall be no more cakes and ale?　　　　*115*

Clown. Yes, by Saint Anne, and ginger° shall be hot
　　i' th' mouth too.

Toby. Th' art i' th' right. —Go, sir, rub your chain
　　with crumbs.° A stoup of wine, Maria!

Malvolio. Mistress Mary, if you prized my lady's favor　*120*
　　at anything more than contempt, you would not
　　give means for this uncivil rule.° She shall know
　　of it, by this hand.　　　　　　　　　　　　　*Exit.*

Maria. Go shake your ears.°

---

102 **Farewell . . . gone** (what follows, in crude antiphony between
Sir Toby and the Clown, is adapted from a ballad, "Corydon's Farewell to Phyllis")　113 **Out o' tune, sir? Ye lie** (Sir Toby accuses the
Clown of being out of tune, it seems, because he had added an extra
"no" and thus an extra note in line 112, and of lying because he had
questioned his valor in "you dare not." Then he turns to berating
Malvolio)　116 **ginger** (commonly used to spice ale)　118–19 **rub
your chain with crumbs** i.e., polish your steward's chain, your badge
of office　122 **give means for this uncivil rule** i.e., provide liquor for
this brawl　124 **Go shake your ears** i.e., like the ass you are (?)

125 *Andrew.* 'Twere as good a deed as to drink when a
     man's ahungry,° to challenge him the field,° and
     then to break promise with him and make a fool
     of him.

     Toby. Do't, knight. I'll write thee a challenge; or I'll
130 deliver thy indignation to him by word of mouth.

     Maria. Sweet Sir Toby, be patient for tonight. Since
     the youth of the Count's was today with my lady,
     she is much out of quiet. For Monsieur Malvolio,
     let me alone with him. If I do not gull him into a
135 nayword,° and make him a common recreation, do
     not think I have wit enough to lie straight in my
     bed. I know I can do it.

     Toby. Possess° us, possess us. Tell us something of
     him.

140 *Maria.* Marry, sir, sometimes he is a kind of Puritan.°

     Andrew. O, if I thought that, I'd beat him like a dog.

     Toby. What, for being a Puritan? Thy exquisite
     reason, dear knight.

     Andrew. I have no exquisite reason for't, but I have
145 reason good enough.

     Maria. The devil a Puritan that he is, or anything
     constantly° but a time-pleaser;° an affectioned° ass,
     that cons state without book° and utters it by great
     swarths;° the best persuaded of himself;° so
150 crammed, as he thinks, with excellencies that it is
     his grounds of faith that all that look on him love
     him; and on that vice in him will my revenge find
     notable cause to work.

126 **ahungry** (characteristically, Sir Andrew confuses hunger and
thirst and thus perverts the proverbial expression)   126 **the field** i.e.,
to a duel   135 **nayword** byword   138 **Possess** inform   140 **Puritan**
i.e., a straight-laced, censorious person (in lines 146–47 Maria makes
it clear that she is not using the label in a strict ecclesiastical sense, as
Sir Andrew [line 141] thinks)   147 **constantly** consistently   147
time-pleaser sycophant   147 **affectioned** affected   148 **cons state**
without book i.e., memorizes stately gestures and turns of phrase
149 **swarths** swaths, quantities   149 **the best persuaded of himself**
i.e., who thinks most highly of himself

Toby. What wilt thou do?

Maria. I will drop in his way some obscure epistles of   *155*
love, wherein by the color of his beard, the shape of
his leg, the manner of his gait, the expressure° of
his eye, forehead, and complexion, he shall find
himself most feelingly personated.° I can write very
like my lady your niece; on a forgotten matter we   *160*
can hardly make distinction of our hands.

Toby. Excellent. I smell a device.

Andrew. I have't in my nose too.

Toby. He shall think by the letters that thou wilt drop
that they come from my niece, and that she's in love   *165*
with him.

Maria. My purpose is indeed a horse of that color.

Andrew. And your horse now would make him an
ass.

Maria. Ass, I doubt not.   *170*

Andrew. O, 'twill be admirable.

Maria. Sport royal, I warrant you. I know my physic
will work with him. I will plant you two, and let
the fool make a third,° where he shall find the
letter. Observe his construction° of it. For this   *175*
night, to bed, and dream on the event.° Farewell.

                                        Exit.

Toby. Good night, Penthesilea.°

Andrew. Before me,° she's a good wench.

Toby. She's a beagle° true-bred, and one that adores
me. What o' that?   *180*

157 **expressure** expression   159 **personated** represented   173–74 **let
the fool make a third** (like the plan to have Viola present herself to
Duke Orsino as a eunuch [I.ii.62], this plot device was abandoned; it
is Fabian, not the Clown, who makes the third spectator to Malvolio's exposé)   175 **construction** interpretation   176 **event** outcome
177 **Penthesilea** (in classical mythology, the queen of the Amazons)
178 **Before me** i.e., I swear, with myself as witness   179 **beagle** (one
of several allusions to Maria's small stature)

Andrew. I was adored once too.

Toby. Let's to bed, knight. Thou hadst need send for more money.

Andrew. If I cannot recover° your niece, I am a foul
185 way out.°

Toby. Send for money, knight. If thou hast her not i' th' end, call me Cut.°

Andrew. If I do not, never trust me, take it how you will.

190 *Toby*. Come, come; I'll go burn some sack.° 'Tis too late to go to bed now. Come, knight; come, knight.

Exeunt.

Scene IV. [*The Duke's palace.*]

Enter Duke, Viola, Curio, and others.

Duke. Give me some music. Now good morrow, friends.
Now, good Cesario, but that piece of song,
That old and antic° song we heard last night.
Methought it did relieve my passion° much,
5   More than light airs and recollected terms°
Of these most brisk and giddy-pacèd times.
Come, but one verse.

Curio. He is not here, so please your lordship, that should sing it.

10 *Duke*. Who was it?

Curio. Feste the jester, my lord, a fool that the Lady

---

184 **recover** win   184–85 **a foul way out** i.e., badly out of pocket
187 **Cut** i.e., a dock-tailed horse   190 **burn some sack** heat and
spice some Spanish wine   II.iv.3 **antic** quaint   4 **passion** suffering
(from unrequited love)   5 **recollected terms** studied phrases

Olivia's father took much delight in. He is about the
house.

Duke. Seek him out, and play the tune the while.
                         [*Exit Curio.*] *Music plays.*
Come hither, boy. If ever thou shalt love,   15
In the sweet pangs of it remember me;
For such as I am all true lovers are,
Unstaid and skittish in all motions° else
Save in the constant image of the creature
That is beloved. How dost thou like this tune?   20

Viola. It gives a very echo to the seat°
Where Love is throned.

Duke.   Thou dost speak masterly.
My life upon't, young though thou art, thine eye
Hath stayed upon some favor° that it loves.
Hath it not, boy?

Viola.   A little, by your favor.   25

Duke. What kind of woman is't?

Viola.   Of your complexion.°

Duke. She is not worth thee then. What years, i' faith?

Viola. About your years, my lord.

Duke. Too old, by heaven. Let still° the woman take
An elder than herself: so wears she° to him,   30
So sways she level in her husband's heart;°
For, boy, however we do praise ourselves,
Our fancies° are more giddy and unfirm,
More longing, wavering, sooner lost and worn,°
Than women's are.

Viola.   I think it well, my lord.   35

Duke. Then let thy love be younger than thyself,

---

18 **motions** emotions   21 **seat** i.e., the heart (see I.i.38–39)   24 **favor**
face   26 **complexion** temperament   29 **still** always   30 **wears she**
she adapts herself   31 **sways she . . . heart** i.e., she keeps steady in
her husband's affections   33 **fancies** loves   34 **worn** (many editors
have adopted the reading "won" from the Second Folio)

Or thy affection cannot hold the bent;°
For women are as roses, whose fair flow'r,
Being once displayed, doth fall that very hour.

40 *Viola.* And so they are; alas, that they are so.
To die, even when they to perfection grow.

Enter Curio and Clown.

Duke. O, fellow, come, the song we had last night.
Mark it, Cesario; it is old and plain.
The spinsters° and the knitters in the sun,
And the free° maids that weave their thread with
45   bones,°
Do use to chant it. It is silly sooth,°
And dallies° with the innocence of love,
Like the old age.°

Clown. Are you ready, sir?

50 *Duke.* I prithee sing.   *Music.*

The Song.

Come away, come away, death,
    And in sad cypress° let me be laid.
Fly away, fly away, breath;
    I am slain by a fair cruel maid.
55 My shroud of white, stuck all with yew,
        O, prepare it.
My part of death, no one so true
        Did share it.

Not a flower, not a flower sweet,
60   On my black coffin let there be strown;
Not a friend, not a friend greet
        My poor corpse, where my bones shall be
            thrown.

37 **hold the bent** i.e., maintain its strength and tension (the image is
that of a bent bow)   44 **spinsters** spinners   45 **free** carefree
45 **bones** i.e., bone bobbins   46 **silly sooth** simple truth   47 **dallies**
deals movingly   48 **the old age** i.e., the good old times   52 **cypress**
a coffin made of cypress wood

   A thousand thousand sighs to save,
     Lay me, O, where
Sad true lover never find my grave,   65
     To weep there.

Duke. There's for thy pains.

Clown. No pains, sir. I take pleasure in singing, sir.

Duke. I'll pay thy pleasure then.

Clown. Truly, sir, and pleasure will be paid one time   70
or another.

Duke. Give me now leave to leave thee.

Clown. Now the melancholy god protect thee, and the
tailor make thy doublet of changeable° taffeta, for
thy mind is a very opal. I would have men of such   75
constancy put to sea, that their business might be
everything, and their intent everywhere; for that's
it that always makes a good voyage of nothing.
Farewell.   *Exit.*

Duke. Let all the rest give place.°
                 [Exeunt Curio and Attendants.]
                    Once more, Cesario,   80
Get thee to yond same sovereign cruelty.°
Tell her my love, more noble than the world,
Prizes not quantity of dirty lands;
The parts° that fortune hath bestowed upon her
Tell her I hold as giddily° as fortune,   85
But 'tis that miracle and queen of gems°
That nature pranks her in° attracts my soul.

Viola. But if she cannot love you, sir?

Duke. I cannot be so answered.

Viola.   Sooth,° but you must.

74 **changeable** i.e., with shifting lights and colors 80 **give place**
withdraw 81 **sovereign cruelty** i.e., peerless and disdainful lady
84 **parts** gifts (of wealth and social status) 85 **giddily** indifferently
86 **queen of gems** i.e., Olivia's beauty 87 **pranks her in** adorns her
with 89 **Sooth** truly

90   Say that some lady, as perhaps there is,
      Hath for your love as great a pang of heart
      As you have for Olivia. You cannot love her.
      You tell her so. Must she not then be answered?

      Duke. There is no woman's sides
95   Can bide° the beating of so strong a passion
      As love doth give my heart; no woman's heart
      So big to hold so much; they lack retention.°
      Alas, their love may be called appetite,
      No motion° of the liver° but the palate,
100   That suffer surfeit, cloyment, and revolt;°
      But mine is all as hungry as the sea
      And can digest as much. Make no compare
      Between that love a woman can bear me
      And that I owe Olivia.

      Viola.   Ay, but I know—

105   *Duke.* What dost thou know?

      Viola. Too well what love women to men may owe.
      In faith, they are as true of heart as we.
      My father had a daughter loved a man
      As it might be perhaps, were I a woman,
      I should your lordship.

110   *Duke.*   And what's her history?

      Viola. A blank, my lord. She never told her love,
      But let concealment, like a worm i' th' bud,
      Feed on her damask° cheek. She pined in thought;°
      And, with a green and yellow melancholy,
115   She sat like Patience on a monument,
      Smiling at grief. Was not this love indeed?
      We men may say more, swear more; but indeed
      Our shows are more than will;° for still we prove
      Much in our vows but little in our love.

120   *Duke.* But died thy sister of her love, my boy?

95 **bide** endure   97 **retention** i.e., the ability to retain   99 **motion**
stirring, prompting   99 **liver** (seat of passion)   100 **revolt** revulsion
113 **damask** i.e., like a pink and white damask rose   113 **thought**
brooding   118 **Our shows are more than will** i.e., what we show is
greater than the passion that we feel

Viola. I am all the daughters of my father's house,
   And all the brothers too, and yet I know not.°
   Sir, shall I to this lady?

Duke.   Ay, that's the theme.
   To her in haste. Give her this jewel. Say
   My love can give no place,° bide no denay.°   *125*
                              Exeunt.

Scene V. [*Olivia's garden.*]

Enter Sir Toby, Sir Andrew, and Fabian.

Toby. Come thy ways, Signior Fabian.

Fabian. Nay, I'll come. If I lose a scruple° of this
   sport, let me be boiled° to death with melancholy.

Toby. Wouldst thou not be glad to have the niggardly
   rascally sheep-biter° come by some notable shame?   *5*

Fabian. I would exult, man. You know he brought me
   out o' favor with my lady about a bearbaiting here.

Toby. To anger him we'll have the bear again, and we
   will fool him black and blue. Shall we not, Sir
   Andrew?   *10*

Andrew. And we do not, it is pity of our lives.

Enter Maria.

Toby. Here comes the little villain. How now, my
   metal of India?°

122 **I know not** (because she thinks that her brother may be still
alive)   125 **can give no place** cannot yield   125 **denay** denial   II.v.2
scruple smallest part   3 **boiled** (pronounced "biled," quibbling on
"bile," which was thought to be the cause of melancholy)   5 **sheep-
biter** i.e., sneaky dog   13 **metal of India** i.e., golden girl

Maria. Get ye all three into the box tree. Malvolio's
15   coming down this walk. He has been yonder i' the
sun practicing behavior to his own shadow this half
hour. Observe him, for the love of mockery; for I
know this letter will make a contemplative° idiot of
of him. Close,° in the name of jesting. [*The others*
20   *hide.*] Lie thou there [*throws down a letter*]; for
here comes the trout that must be caught with
tickling.°   *Exit.*

Enter Malvolio.

Malvolio. 'Tis but fortune; all is fortune. Maria once
told me she did affect me;° and I have heard herself
25   come thus near, that, should she fancy,° it should
be one of my complexion. Besides, she uses me with
a more exalted respect than anyone else that
follows° her. What should I think on't?

Toby. Here's an overweening rogue.

30 *Fabian.* O, peace! Contemplation makes a rare turkey
cock of him. How he jets° under his advanced°
plumes!

Andrew. 'Slight,° I could so beat the rogue.

Toby. Peace, I say.°

35 *Malvolio.* To be Count Malvolio.

Toby. Ah, rogue!

Andrew. Pistol him, pistol him.

Toby. Peace, peace.

Malvolio. There is example for't. The Lady of the
40   Strachy° married the yeoman of the wardrobe.

18 **contemplative** i.e., self-centered   19 **Close** hide   22 **tickling**
stroking, i.e., flattery   24 **she did affect me** i.e., Olivia liked me
25 **fancy** love   28 **follows** serves   31 **jets** struts   31 **advanced** up-
lifted   33 **'Slight** by God's light (a mild oath)   34 **Peace, I say**
(many editors assign this and line 38 to Fabian on the ground that
it is his function throughout the scene to restrain Sir Toby and Sir
Andrew)   39–40 **The Lady of the Strachy** (an unidentified allusion
to a great lady who married beneath her)

Andrew. Fie on him, Jezebel.°

Fabian. O, peace! Now he's deeply in. Look how imagination blows him.°

Malvolio. Having been three months married to her, sitting in my state—   45

Toby. O for a stonebow,° to hit him in the eye!

Malvolio. Calling my officers about me, in my branched° velvet gown; having come from a day-bed,° where I have left Olivia sleeping—

Toby. Fire and brimstone!   50

Fabian. O, peace, peace!

Malvolio. And then to have the humor of state;° and after a demure travel of regard,° telling them I know my place, as I would they should do theirs, to ask for my kinsman Toby—   55

Toby. Bolts and shackles!

Fabian. O peace, peace, peace, now, now.

Malvolio. Seven of my people, with an obedient start, make out for° him. I frown the while, and perchance wind up my watch, or play with my—some   60
rich jewel.° Toby approaches; curtsies there to me—

Toby. Shall this fellow live?

Fabian. Though our silence be drawn from us with cars, yet peace.

Malvolio. I extend my hand to him thus, quenching   65
my familiar smile with an austere regard of control°—

41 **Jezebel** (the proud and wicked queen of Ahab, King of Israel, whom Sir Andrew, muddled as usual, regards as Malvolio's proto-type in arrogance) 43 **blows him** puffs him up 46 **stonebow** crossbow that shoots stones 48 **branched** embroidered 48–49 **daybed** sofa 52 **to have the humor of state** i.e., to assume an imperious manner 53 **after a demure travel of regard** i.e., having glanced gravely over my retainers 59 **make out for** i.e., go to fetch 60–61 **play with my—some rich jewel** (Malvolio automatically reaches for his steward's chain and then catches himself) 66–67 **an austere regard of control** i.e., a stern look of authority

Toby. And does not Toby take° you a blow o' the
lips then?

70 *Malvolio.* Saying, "Cousin Toby, my fortunes having
cast me on your niece, give me this prerogative of
speech."

Toby. What, what?

Malvolio. "You must amend your drunkenness."

75 *Toby.* Out, scab!

Fabian. Nay, patience, or we break the sinews of our
plot.

Malvolio. "Besides, you waste the treasure of your
time with a foolish knight"—

80 *Andrew.* That's me, I warrant you.

Malvolio. "One Sir Andrew"—

Andrew. I knew 'twas I, for many do call me fool.

Malvolio. What employment° have we here?
                                    [*Takes up the letter.*]

Fabian. Now is the woodcock° near the gin.°

85 *Toby.* O, peace, and the spirit of humors intimate
reading aloud to him!

Malvolio. By my life, this is my lady's hand. These be
her very C's, her U's, and her T's; and thus makes
she her great P's. It is, in contempt of° question,
90 her hand.

Andrew. Her C's, her U's, and her T's? Why that?

Malvolio. [*Reads*] "To the unknown beloved, this,
and my good wishes." Her very phrases! By your
leave, wax.° Soft,° and the impressure her Lucrece,°

68 **take** give   83 **employment** business   84 **woodcock** (a proverbially
stupid bird)   84 **gin** snare   89 **in contempt of** beyond   93–94 **By
your leave, wax** i.e., excuse me for breaking the seal   94 **Soft** i.e.,
take it slowly   94 **the impressure her Lucrece** i.e., the seal depicts
Lucrece (noble Roman matron who stabbed herself after she was
raped by Tarquin, hence a symbol of chastity)

with which she uses to seal.° 'Tis my lady. To   95
whom should this be?

Fabian. This wins him, liver and all.

Malvolio. [*Reads*]
                "Jove knows I love,
                    But who?
                Lips, do not move;
                    No man must know."   100
"No man must know." What follows? The numbers
altered!° "No man must know." If this should be
thee, Malvolio?

Toby. Marry, hang thee, brock!°
                                            105

Malvolio. [*Reads*]
    "I may command where I adore,
        But silence, like a Lucrece knife,
    With bloodless stroke my heart doth gore.
        M. O. A. I. doth sway my life."

Fabian. A fustian° riddle.
                                            110

Toby. Excellent wench,° say I.

Malvolio. "M. O. A. I. doth sway my life." Nay, but
first, let me see, let me see, let me see.

Fabian. What dish o' poison has she dressed° him!

Toby. And with what wing the staniel checks at it!°   115

Malvolio. "I may command where I adore." Why, she
may command me: I serve her; she is my lady.
Why, this is evident to any formal capacity.° There
is no obstruction° in this. And the end; what should
that alphabetical position portend? If I could make   120
that resemble something in me! Softly, "M. O. A. I."

Toby. O, ay, make up that. He is now at a cold scent.

95 **uses to seal** customarily seals   102–103 **The numbers altered** the
meter changed (in the stanza that follows)   105 **brock** badger
110 **fustian** i.e., foolish and pretentious   111 **wench** i.e., Maria
114 **dressed** prepared for   115 **with what wing the staniel checks at
it** i.e., with what speed the kestrel (a kind of hawk) turns to snatch
at the wrong prey   118 **formal capacity** normal intelligence   119
obstruction difficulty

Fabian. Sowter will cry upon't for all this, though it
be as rank as a fox.°

125 *Malvolio.* M.—Malvolio. M.—Why, that begins my
name.

Fabian. Did not I say he would work it out? The cur
is excellent at faults.°

Malvolio. M.—But then there is no consonancy in the
130   sequel.° That suffers under probation.° A should
follow, but O does.

Fabian. And O° shall end, I hope.

Toby. Ay, or I'll cudgel him, and make him cry O.

Malvolio. And then I comes behind.

135 *Fabian.* Ay, and you had any eye behind you, you
might see more detraction at your heels than
fortunes before you.

Malvolio. M, O, A, I. This simulation° is not as the
former; and yet, to crush° this a little, it would bow
140   to me, for every one of these letters are in my name.
Soft, here follows prose.

[*Reads*] "If this fall into thy hand, revolve.° In my
stars° I am above thee, but be not afraid of greatness. Some are born great, some achieve greatness,
145   and some have greatness thrust upon 'em. Thy
Fates open their hands; let thy blood and spirit
embrace them; and to inure° thyself to what thou
art like to be, cast thy humble slough° and appear
fresh. Be opposite with° a kinsman, surly with
150   servants. Let thy tongue tang arguments of state;°
put thyself into the trick of singularity.° She thus

123–24 **Sowter will cry . . . as a fox** i.e., the hound will bay after the
false scent even though the deceit is gross and clear   128 **faults**
breaks in the scent   129–30 **consonancy in the sequel** consistency
in what follows   130 **suffers under probation** does not stand up
under scrutiny   132 **O** i.e., sound of lamentation   138 **simulation**
hidden significance   139 **crush** force   142 **revolve** reflect   143 **stars**
fortune   147 **inure** accustom   148 **slough** skin (of a snake)   149
opposite with hostile to   150 **tang arguments of state** i.e., resound
with topics of statecraft   151 **trick of singularity** affectation of
eccentricity

advises thee that sighs for thee. Remember who
commended thy yellow stockings and wished to see
thee ever cross-gartered.° I say, remember. Go to,
thou art made, if thou desir'st to be so. If not, let　155
me see thee a steward still, the fellow of servants,
and not worthy to touch Fortune's fingers. Farewell.
She that would alter services with thee,
　　　　THE FORTUNATE UNHAPPY."

Daylight and champian° discovers° not more. This　160
is open. I will be proud, I will read politic authors,°
I will baffle° Sir Toby, I will wash off gross° acquaintance, I will be point-devise,° the very man.
I do not now fool myself, to let imagination jade°
me, for every reason excites to this,° that my lady　165
loves me. She did commend my yellow stockings of
late, she did praise my leg being cross-gartered; and
in this she manifests herself to my love, and with
a kind of injunction drives me to these habits of her
liking.° I thank my stars, I am happy. I will be　170
strange,° stout,° in yellow stockings, and cross-
gartered, even with the swiftness of putting on. Jove
and my stars be praised. Here is yet a postscript.
[Reads] "Thou canst not choose but know who I
am. If thou entertain'st° my love, let it appear in　175
thy smiling. Thy smiles become thee well. Therefore in my presence still smile, dear my sweet, I
prithee."
Jove, I thank thee. I will smile; I will do everything
that thou wilt have me.　　　　　　　Exit.　180

Fabian. I will not give my part of this sport for a
pension of thousands to be paid from the Sophy.°

154 **cross-gartered** i.e., with garters crossed above and below the
knee　160 **champian** champaign, open country　160 **discovers** reveals　161 **politic authors** writers on politics　162 **baffle** publicly
humiliate　162 **gross** low　163 **be point-devise** i.e., follow the advice
in the letter in every detail　164 **jade** trick　165 **excites to this**
i.e., enforces this conclusion　169–170 **these habits of her liking**
this clothing that she likes　171 **strange** haughty　171 **stout** proud
175 **entertain'st** accept　182 **Sophy** Shah of Persia (perhaps with
reference to Sir Anthony Shirley's visit to the Persian court in 1599,
from which he returned laden with gifts and honors)

Toby. I could marry this wench for this device.

Andrew. So could I too.

185 *Toby.* And ask no other dowry with her but such another jest.

Enter Maria.

Andrew. Nor I neither.

Fabian. Here comes my noble gull-catcher.°

Toby. Wilt thou set thy foot o' my neck?

190 *Andrew.* Or o' mine either?

Toby. Shall I play° my freedom at tray-trip° and become thy bondslave?

Andrew. I' faith, or I either?

Toby. Why, thou hast put him in such a dream that,
195 when the image of it leaves him, he must run mad.

Maria. Nay, but say true, does it work upon him?

Toby. Like aqua-vitae° with a midwife.

Maria. If you will, then, see the fruits of the sport, mark his first approach before my lady. He will
200 come to her in yellow stockings, and 'tis a color she abhors, and cross-gartered, a fashion she detests; and he will smile upon her which will now be so unsuitable to her disposition, being addicted to a melancholy as she is, that it cannot but turn him
205 into a notable contempt. If you will see it, follow me.

Toby. To the gates of Tartar,° thou most excellent devil of wit.

Andrew. I'll make one° too.   *Exeunt.*

188 **gull-catcher** fool-catcher   191 **play** gamble   191 **tray-trip** (a dice game)   197 **aqua-vitae** distilled liquors   207 **Tartar** Tartarus (in classical mythology, the infernal regions)   209 **make one** i.e., come

ACT III

Scene I. [*Olivia's garden.*]

Enter Viola and Clown [with a tabor].

Viola. Save thee,° friend, and thy music. Dost thou
live by° thy tabor?°

Clown. No, sir, I live by the church.

Viola. Art thou a churchman?

Clown. No such matter, sir. I do live by the church;   5
for I do live at my house, and my house doth stand
by the church.

Viola. So thou mayst say, the king lies° by a beggar,
if a beggar dwell near him; or, the church stands
by° thy tabor, if thy tabor stand by the church.   10

Clown. You have said, sir. To see this age! A sentence is but a chev'ril° glove to a good wit. How
quickly the wrong side may be turned outward!

Viola. Nay, that's certain. They that dally nicely°
with words may quickly make them wanton.°   15

Clown. I would therefore my sister had had no name,
sir.

III.i.1 **Save thee** i.e., God save you   2 **live by** gain a living from (but
the Clown takes it in the sense of "reside near")   2 **tabor** (1) drum
(2) taborn, tavern   8 **lies** sojourns   9-10 **stands by** (1) stands near
(2) upholds   12 **chev'ril** cheveril (i.e., soft kid leather)   14 **dally
nicely** play subtly   15 **wanton** i.e., equivocal in meaning (but the
Clown takes it in the sense of "unchaste")

Viola. Why, man?

Clown. Why, sir, her name's a word, and to dally with
20   that word might make my sister wanton. But indeed
words are very rascals since bonds disgraced them.°

Viola. Thy reason, man?

Clown. Troth,° sir, I can yield you none without
words, and words are grown so false I am loath to
25   prove reason with them.

Viola. I warrant thou art a merry fellow and car'st
for nothing.

Clown. Not so, sir; I do care for something; but in my
conscience, sir, I do not care for you. If that be to
30   care for nothing, sir, I would it would make you
invisible.

Viola. Art not thou the Lady Olivia's fool?

Clown. No, indeed, sir. The Lady Olivia has no folly.
She will keep no fool, sir, till she be married; and
35   fools are as like husbands as pilchers° are to herrings—the husband's the bigger. I am indeed not
her fool, but her corrupter of words.

Viola. I saw thee late at the Count Orsino's.

Clown. Foolery, sir, does walk about the orb° like
40   the sun; it shines everywhere. I would be sorry, sir,
but° the fool should be as oft with your master as
with my mistress. I think I saw your wisdom there.

Viola. Nay, and thou pass upon me,° I'll no more
with thee. Hold, there's expenses for thee.

[*Gives a coin.*]

45   *Clown.* Now Jove, in his next commodity° of hair,
send thee a beard.

21 **since bonds disgraced them** i.e., since it was required that a man's
word be guaranteed by a bond (?)   23 **Troth** by my troth
35 **pilchers** pilchards (a kind of small herring)   39 **orb** earth
41 **but** but that   43 **pass upon me** i.e., make me the butt of your
witticisms   45 **commodity** lot, consignment

Viola. By my troth, I'll tell thee, I am almost sick
  for one, though I would not have it grow on my
  chin. Is thy lady within?

Clown. Would not a pair of these° have bred, sir?   50

Viola. Yes, being kept together and put to use.°

Clown. I would play Lord Pandarus of Phrygia, sir,
  to bring a Cressida to this Troilus.°

Viola. I understand you, sir. 'Tis well begged.
                          [*Gives another coin.*]

Clown. The matter, I hope, is not great, sir, begging   55
  but a beggar: Cressida was a beggar.° My lady is
  within, sir. I will conster° to them whence you
  come. Who you are and what you would are out of
  my welkin;° I might say "element," but the word is
  overworn.°   *Exit.*   60

Viola. This fellow is wise enough to play the fool,
  And to do that well craves° a kind of wit.°
  He must observe their mood on whom he jests,
  The quality of persons, and the time;
  And,° like the haggard,° check at° every feather   65
  That comes before his eye. This is a practice°
  As full of labor as a wise man's art;
  For folly that he wisely shows, is fit;
  But wise men, folly-fall'n,° quite taint their wit.°

---

50 **these** i.e., coins of the sort that Viola had just given him   51 **put
to use** put out at interest   52–53 **I would play . . . this Troilus** (in
the story of Troilus and Cressida, which supplied both Chaucer and
Shakespeare the plot for major works, Pandarus was the go-between
in the disastrous love affair)   56 **Cressida was a beggar** (in Robert
Henryson's *Testament of Cressida*, a kind of sequel to Chaucer's
poem, the faithless heroine became a harlot and a beggar)
57 **conster** explain   59 **welkin** sky   59–60 **I might say . . . overworn**
(perhaps a thrust at Ben Jonson, whose fondness for the word "element" had been ridiculed by other writers)   62 **craves** requires
62 **wit** intelligence   65 **And** (many editors, following Johnson, have
emended this to "not")   65 **haggard** untrained hawk   65 **check at**
leave the true course and pursue   66 **practice** skill   69 **folly-fall'n**
having fallen into folly   69 **taint their wit** i.e., betray their common
sense

Enter Sir Toby and [Sir] Andrew.

70 *Toby.* Save you, gentleman.

Viola. And you, sir.

Andrew. Dieu vous garde, monsieur.

Viola. Et vous aussi; votre serviteur.°

Andrew. I hope, sir, you are, and I am yours.

75 *Toby.* Will you encounter° the house? My niece is
   desirous you should enter, if your trade be to° her.

Viola. I am bound to° your niece, sir; I mean, she is
   the list° of my voyage.

Toby. Taste° your legs, sir; put them to motion.

80 *Viola.* My legs do better understand° me, sir, than I
   understand what you mean by bidding me taste my
   legs.

Toby. I mean, to go, sir, to enter.

Viola. I will answer you with gait and entrance.° But
85 we are prevented.°

   Enter Olivia and Gentlewoman [Maria].

   Most excellent accomplished lady, the heavens rain
   odors on you.

Andrew. That youth's a rare courtier. "Rain odors"—
   well!°

90 *Viola.* My matter hath no voice,° lady, but to your
   own most pregnant and vouchsafed ear.

72–73 **Dieu vous garde ... votre serviteur** God protect you, sir./And
you also; your servant   75 **encounter** approach   76 **trade be to**
business be with   77 **bound to** bound for (carrying on the metaphor
in "trade")   78 **list** destination   79 **Taste** try   80 **understand** i.e.,
stand under, support   84 **with gait and entrance** by going and enter-
ing (with a pun on "gate")   85 **prevented** anticipated   89 **well**
i.e., well put   90 **matter hath no voice** i.e., business must not be
revealed

Andrew. "Odors," "pregnant," and "vouchsafed"—
I'll get 'em all three all ready.

Olivia. Let the garden door be shut, and leave me to
my hearing. [*Exeunt Sir Toby, Sir Andrew, and*   95
Maria.] Give me your hand, sir.

Viola. My duty, madam, and most humble service.

Olivia. What is your name?

Viola. Cesario is your servant's name, fair princess.

Olivia. My servant, sir? 'Twas never merry world   100
Since lowly feigning° was called compliment.
Y' are servant to the Count Orsino, youth.

Viola. And he is yours, and his must needs be yours.
Your servant's servant is your servant, madam.

Olivia. For° him, I think not on him; for his thoughts,   105
Would they were blanks, rather than filled with me.

Viola. Madam, I come to whet your gentle thoughts
On his behalf.

Olivia.   O, by your leave, I pray you.
I bade you never speak again of him;
But, would you undertake another suit,
I had rather hear you to solicit that   110
Than music from the spheres.°

Viola.   Dear lady—

Olivia. Give me leave,° beseech you. I did send,
After the last enchantment you did here,
A ring in chase of you. So did I abuse°   115
Myself, my servant, and, I fear me, you.
Under your hard construction° must I sit,
To force that on you in a shameful cunning
Which you knew none of yours. What might you
   think?

---

101 **lowly feigning** affected humility 105 **For** as for 112 **music
from the spheres** i.e., the alleged celestial harmony of the revolving
stars and planets 113 **Give me leave** i.e., do not interrupt me
115 **abuse** deceive 117 **hard construction** harsh interpretation

120 Have you not set mine honor at the stake
And baited it with all th' unmuzzled thoughts°
That tyrannous heart can think? To one of your
    receiving°
Enough is shown; a cypress,° not a bosom,
Hides my heart. So, let me hear you speak.

Viola. I pity you.

125 *Olivia.*   That's a degree° to love.

Viola. No, not a grize;° for 'tis a vulgar proof°
That very oft we pity enemies.

Olivia. Why then, methinks 'tis time to smile again.
O world, how apt the poor are to be proud.
130 If one should be a prey, how much the better
To fall before the lion than the wolf.   *Clock strikes.*
The clock upbraids me with the waste of time.
Be not afraid, good youth, I will not have you,
And yet, when wit and youth is come to harvest,°
135 Your wife is like to reap a proper° man.
There lies your way, due west.°

Viola.   Then westward ho!°
Grace and good disposition° attend your ladyship.
You'll nothing, madam, to my lord by me?

Olivia. Stay.
140 I prithee tell me what thou think'st of me.

Viola. That you do think you are not what you are.°

Olivia. If I think so, I think the same of you.°

120–121 **set mine honor . . . unmuzzled thoughts** (the metaphor is
from the Elizabethan sport of bearbaiting, in which a bear was tied
to a stake and harassed by savage dogs)   122 **receiving** i.e., per-
ception   123 **cypress** gauzelike material   125 **degree** step   126 **grize**
step   126 **vulgar proof** i.e., common knowledge   134 **when wit and
youth is come to harvest** i.e., when you are mature   135 **proper**
handsome   136 **due west** (Olivia is perhaps implying that the sun
of her life—Cesario's love—is about to vanish)   136 **westward ho**
(cry of Thames watermen)   137 **good disposition** i.e., tranquillity
of mind   141 **That you do think you are not what you are** i.e., that
you think you are in love with a man, and are not   142 **If I think
so, I think the same of you** (Olivia misconstrues Viola's remark to
mean that she is out of her mind)

Viola. Then think you right. I am not what I am.

Olivia. I would you were as I would have you be.

Viola. Would it be better, madam, than I am?   *145*
    I wish it might, for now I am your fool.°

Olivia. O, what a deal of scorn looks beautiful
    In the contempt and anger of his lip.
    A murd'rous guilt shows not itself more soon
    Than love that would seem hid: love's night is
       noon.°   *150*
    Cesario, by the roses of the spring,
    By maidhood,° honor, truth, and everything,
    I love thee so that, maugre° all thy pride,
    Nor wit nor reason can my passion hide.
    Do not extort thy reasons from this clause,°   *155*
    For that° I woo, thou therefore hast no cause;°
    But rather reason thus with reason fetter,
    Love sought is good, but given unsought is better.

Viola. By innocence I swear, and by my youth,
    I have one heart, one bosom, and one truth,   *160*
    And that no woman has; nor never none
    Shall mistress be of it, save I alone.
    And so adieu, good madam. Never more
    Will I my master's tears to you deplore.

Olivia. Yet come again; for thou perhaps mayst move   *165*
    That heart which now abhors to like his love.

                               Exeunt.

---

146 **I am your fool** i.e., you are making a fool of me   150 **love's
night is noon** i.e., love is apparent even when it is hidden   152 **maid-
hood** maidenhood   153 **maugre** despite   155 **clause** premise   156
For that that because   156 **cause** i.e., to accept my love

Scene II. [*Olivia's house.*]

Enter Sir Toby, Sir Andrew, and Fabian.

Andrew. No, faith, I'll not stay a jot longer.

Toby. Thy reason, dear venom; give thy reason.

Fabian. You must needs yield° your reason, Sir Andrew.

5   *Andrew.* Marry, I saw your niece do more favors to the Count's servingman than ever she bestowed upon me. I saw't i' th' orchard.

Toby. Did she see thee the while, old boy? Tell me that.

10 *Andrew.* As plain as I see you now.

Fabian. This was a great argument° of love in her toward you.

Andrew. 'Slight, will you make an ass o' me?

Fabian. I will prove it legitimate,° sir, upon the oaths
15 of judgment and reason.

Toby. And they have been grand-jurymen since before Noah was a sailor.

Fabian. She did show favor to the youth in your sight only to exasperate you, to awake your dormouse°
20 valor, to put fire in your heart and brimstone in your liver. You should then have accosted her, and with some excellent jests, fire-new from the mint, you should have banged the youth into dumbness. This was looked for at your hand, and this was

III.ii.3 **yield** give   11 **great argument** strong evidence   14 **legitimate**
valid   19 **dormouse** i.e., sleepy

balked.° The double gilt° of this opportunity you   *25*
let time wash off, and you are now sailed into the
North of my lady's opinion,° where you will hang
like an icicle on a Dutchman's beard° unless you do
redeem it by some laudable attempt either of valor
or policy.°   *30*

Andrew. And't be any way, it must be with valor; for
policy I hate. I had as lief be a Brownist° as a
politician.°

Toby. Why then, build me thy fortunes upon the basis
of valor. Challenge me the Count's youth to fight   *35*
with him; hurt him in eleven places. My niece shall
take note of it, and assure thyself there is no love-
broker in the world can° more prevail in man's
commendation with woman than report of valor.

Fabian. There is no way but this, Sir Andrew.   *40*

Andrew. Will either of you bear me a challenge to
him?

Toby. Go, write it in a martial hand. Be curst° and
brief; it is no matter how witty, so it be eloquent
and full of invention. Taunt him with the license of *45*
ink.° If thou thou'st° him some thrice, it shall not
be amiss; and as many lies as will lie in thy sheet
of paper, although the sheet were big enough for
the bed of Ware° in England, set 'em down. Go
about it. Let there be gall enough in thy ink, though *50*
thou write with a goose-pen, no matter. About it!

Andrew. Where shall I find you?

---

25 **balked** let slip   25 **gilt** plating   26–27 **the North of my lady's opinion** i.e., her frosty disdain   28 **an icicle on a Dutchman's beard** (perhaps an allusion to the arctic voyage [1596–97] of the Dutchman Willem Barents, an account of which was registered for publication in 1598)   30 **policy** intrigue, trickery   32 **Brownist** follower of William Browne, a reformer who advocated the separation of church and state   33 **politician** schemer   38 **can** i.e., that can   43 **curst** petulant   45–46 **the license of ink** i.e., the freedom that writing permits   46 **thou'st** i.e., use the familiar "thou" instead of the more formal "you"   49 **the bed of Ware** a famous bedstead, almost eleven feet square, formerly in an inn at Ware in Herfordshire

Toby. We'll call thee at the cubiculo.° Go.

                               Exit Sir Andrew.

Fabian. This is a dear manikin° to you, Sir Toby.

55 *Toby.* I have been dear to him,° lad, some two thousand strong or so.

Fabian. We shall have a rare letter from him, but
you'll not deliver't?

Toby. Never trust me then; and by all means stir on
60   the youth to an answer. I think oxen and wain-
ropes° cannot hale them together. For Andrew,
if he were opened, and you find so much blood in
his liver as will clog the foot of a flea, I'll eat the
rest of th' anatomy.°

65 *Fabian.* And his opposite,° the youth, bears in his
visage no great presage of cruelty.

                   Enter Maria.

Toby. Look where the youngest wren° of mine° comes.

Maria. If you desire the spleen,° and will laugh yourselves into stitches, follow me. Yond gull Malvolio
70   is turned heathen, a very renegado; for there is no
Christian that means to be saved by believing
rightly can ever believe such impossible passages
of grossness.° He's in yellow stockings.

Toby. And cross-gartered?

75 *Maria.* Most villainously; like a pedant that keeps a
school i' th' church. I have dogged him like his
murderer. He does obey every point of the letter
that I dropped to betray him. He does smile his
face into more lines than is in the new map with

53 **cubiculo** little chamber   54 **manikin** puppet   55 **been dear to
him** i.e., spent his money   60–61 **wainropes** wagon ropes   64 **anatomy** cadaver   65 **opposite** adversary   67 **youngest wren** i.e., smallest of small birds   67 **mine** (most editors adopt Theobald's emendation "nine")   68 **spleen** i.e., a fit of laughter   72–73 **impossible
passages of grossness** i.e., improbabilities

the augmentation of the Indies.° You have not seen   80
such a thing as 'tis. I can hardly forbear hurling
things at him. I know my lady will strike him. If
she do, he'll smile, and take't for a great favor.

Toby. Come bring us, bring us where he is.

                                        Exeunt omnes.

Scene III. [*A street.*]

Enter Sebastian and Antonio.

Sebastian. I would not by my will have troubled you;
    But since you make your pleasure of your pains,
    I will no further chide you.

Antonio. I could not stay behind you. My desire
    (More sharp than filèd steel) did spur me forth;   5
    And not all love to see you (though so much
    As might have drawn one to a longer voyage)
    But jealousy° what might befall your travel,
    Being skilless in° these parts; which to a stranger,
    Unguided and unfriended, often prove   10
    Rough and unhospitable. My willing love,
    The rather by these arguments of fear,°
    Set forth in your pursuit.

Sebastian.   My kind Antonio,
    I can no other answer make but thanks,
    And thanks, and ever oft good turns°   15

79–80 **the new map with the augmentation of the Indies** (presumably a map, prepared under the supervision of Richard Hakluyt and
others and published about 1600, that employed the principles of
projection and showed North America and the East Indies in fuller
detail than any earlier map. It was conspicuous for the rhumb lines
marking the meridians)   III.iii.8 **jealousy** anxiety   9 **skilless in**
unacquainted with   12 **The rather by these arguments of fear** i.e.,
reinforced by my solicitude for your safety   15 **And thanks, and
ever oft good turns** (the fact that this line is a foot too short has
prompted a wide variety of emendations, the most popular of which
has been Theobald's "And thanks, and ever thanks; and oft good
turns." Later Folios omit this and the following line altogether)

Are shuffled off with such uncurrent° pay.
But, were my worth° as is my conscience firm,
You should find better dealing. What's to do?
Shall we go see the relics of this town?

20 *Antonio.* Tomorrow, sir; best first go see your lodging.

Sebastian. I am not weary, and 'tis long to night.
I pray you let us satisfy our eyes
With the memorials and the things of fame
That do renown this city.

Antonio.   Would you'ld pardon° me.
25 I do not without danger walk these streets.
Once in a sea-fight 'gainst the Count his galleys°
I did some service; of such note indeed
That, were I ta'en here, it would scarce be answered.°

Sebastian. Belike you slew great number of his people?

30 *Antonio.* Th' offense is not of such a bloody nature,
Albeit the quality° of the time and quarrel
Might well have given us bloody argument.°
It might have since been answered° in repaying
What we took from them, which for traffic's° sake
35 Most of our city did. Only myself stood out;
For which, if I be lapsèd° in this place,
I shall pay dear.

Sebastian.   Do not then walk too open.

Antonio. It doth not fit me. Hold, sir, here's my purse.
In the south suburbs at the Elephant°
40 Is best to lodge. I will bespeak our diet,°
Whiles° you beguile the time and feed your knowledge
With viewing of the town. There shall you have°
me.

16 **uncurrent** worthless   17 **worth** resources   24 **pardon** excuse
26 **the Count his galleys** the Count's warships   28 **answered** defended   31 **quality** circumstances   32 **argument** cause   33 **answered** compensated   34 **traffic's** trade's   36 **lapsèd** surprised and apprehended   39 **Elephant** an inn   40 **bespeak our diet** i.e., arrange for our meals   41 **Whiles** while   42 **have** find

Sebastian. Why I your purse?

Antonio. Haply your eye shall light upon some toy°
You have desire to purchase, and your store°   45
I think is not for idle markets,° sir.

Sebastian. I'll be your purse-bearer, and leave you for
An hour.

Antonio.   To th' Elephant.

Sebastian.   I do remember.   *Exeunt.*

Scene IV. [*Olivia's garden.*]

Enter Olivia and Maria.

Olivia. I have sent after him. He says he'll come:°
How shall I feast him? What bestow of° him?
For youth is bought more oft than begged or bor-
     rowed.
I speak too loud. Where's Malvolio? He is sad and
     civil,°
And suits well for a servant with my fortunes.   5
Where is Malvolio?

Maria. He's coming, madam, but in very strange manner. He is sure possessed,° madam.

Olivia. Why, what's the matter? Does he rave?

Maria. No, madam, he does nothing but smile. Your   10
ladyship were best to have some guard about you
if he come, for sure the man is tainted in 's wits.

Olivia. Go call him hither. I am as mad as he,
If sad and merry madness equal be.

44 **toy** trifle   45 **store** wealth   46 **idle markets** unnecessary pur-
chases   III.iv.1 **He says he'll come** suppose he says he'll come   2 **of**
on   4 **sad and civil** grave and formal   8 **possessed** i.e., with a devil,
mad

Enter Malvolio.

15   How now, Malvolio?

Malvolio. Sweet lady, ho, ho!

Olivia. Smil'st thou? I sent for thee upon a sad° occasion.

Malvolio. Sad, lady? I could be sad. This does make
20   some obstruction in the blood, this cross-gartering;
but what of that? If it please the eye of one, it is
with me as the very true sonnet° is, "Please one,
and please all."°

Olivia. Why, how dost thou, man? What is the matter
25   with thee?

Malvolio. Not black in my mind, though yellow in my
legs. It did come to his hands, and commands shall
be executed. I think we do know the sweet Roman
hand.°

30   *Olivia.* Wilt thou go to bed, Malvolio?

Malvolio. To bed? Ay, sweetheart, and I'll come to
thee.

Olivia. God comfort thee. Why dost thou smile so,
and kiss thy hand so oft?

35   *Maria.* How do you, Malvolio?

Malvolio. At your request? Yes, nightingales answer
daws!°

Maria. Why appear you with this ridiculous boldness
before my lady?

40   *Malvolio.* "Be not afraid of greatness." 'Twas well writ.

17 **sad** serious   22 **sonnet** (any short lyric poem)   22–23 **Please
one, and please all** i.e., so long as I please the one I love I do not
care about the rest (from "A prettie newe Ballad, intytuled: The
Crow sits vpon the wall, Please one and please all")   28–29 **the
sweet Roman hand** i.e., italic writing, an elegant cursive script more
fashionable than the crabbed "secretary hand" commonly used in
Shakespeare's time   36–37 **At . . . daws** i.e., should I reply to a
mere servant like you? Yes, for sometimes nightingales answer jack-
daws

Olivia. What mean'st thou by that, Malvolio?

Malvolio. "Some are born great."

Olivia. Ha?

Malvolio. "Some achieve greatness."

Olivia. What say'st thou?   45

Malvolio. "And some have greatness thrust upon them."

Olivia. Heaven restore thee!

Malvolio. "Remember who commended thy yellow stockings."   50

Olivia. Thy yellow stockings?

Malvolio. "And wished to see thee cross-gartered."

Olivia. Cross-gartered?

Malvolio. "Go to, thou art made, if thou desir'st to be so."   55

Olivia. Am I made?

Malvolio. "If not, let me see thee a servant still."

Olivia. Why, this is very midsummer madness.°

Enter Servant.

Servant. Madam, the young gentleman of the Count Orsino's is returned. I could hardly entreat him   60
back. He attends your ladyship's pleasure.

Olivia. I'll come to him. [*Exit Servant.*] Good Maria, let this fellow be looked to. Where's my cousin Toby? Let some of my people have a special care of him. I would not have him miscarry° for the   65
half of my dowry.

Exit [Olivia, accompanied by Maria].

58 **midsummer madness** extreme folly, Midsummer Eve (June 23)
being traditionally associated with irresponsible and eccentric behavior   65 **miscarry** come to harm

Malvolio. O ho, do you come near me° now? No
worse man than Sir Toby to look to me. This con-
curs directly with the letter. She sends him on pur-
70 pose, that I may appear stubborn° to him; for she
incites me to that in the letter. "Cast thy humble
slough," says she; "be opposite with a kinsman,
surly with servants; let thy tongue tang with arguments of state; put thyself into the trick of singu-
75 larity." And consequently sets down the manner
how: as, a sad face, a reverend carriage, a slow
tongue, in the habit° of some sir° of note, and so
forth. I have limed° her; but it is Jove's doing, and
Jove make me thankful. And when she went away
80 now, "Let this fellow° be looked to." "Fellow."
Not "Malvolio," nor after my degree,° but "fellow." Why, everything adheres together, that no
dram° of a scruple,° no scruple of a scruple, no
obstacle, no incredulous or unsafe° circumstance—
85 what can be said? Nothing that can be can come
between me and the full prospect of my hopes.
Well, Jove, not I, is the doer of this, and he is to
be thanked.

Enter [Sir] Toby, Fabian, and Maria.

Toby. Which way is he, in the name of sanctity? If
90 all the devils of hell be drawn in little,° and
Legion° himself possessed him, yet I'll speak to
him.

Fabian. Here he is, here he is! How is't with you, sir?

---

67 **come near me** i.e., begin to understand my importance   70 **stubborn** hostile   77 **habit** clothing   77 **sir** personage   78 **limed** caught
(as birds are caught with sticky birdlime)   80 **fellow** (1) menial
(2) associate (the sense in which Malvolio takes the word)   81 **after
my degree** according to my status   83 **dram** (1) minute part (2)
apothecary's measure for one-eighth of an ounce   83 **scruple** (1)
doubt (2) apothecary's measure for one-third of a dram   84 **incredulous or unsafe** incredible or doubtful   90 **in little** in small
compass   91 **Legion** a group of devils (see Mark 5:8–9)

Toby. How is't with you, man?°

Malvolio. Go off; I discard you. Let me enjoy my   95
private.° Go off.

Maria. Lo, how hollow the fiend speaks within him!
Did not I tell you? Sir Toby, my lady prays you
to have a care of him.

Malvolio. Aha, does she so?   100

Toby. Go to, go to; peace, peace; we must deal gently
with him. Let me alone. How do you, Malvolio?
How is't with you? What, man, defy the devil?
Consider, he's an enemy to mankind.

Malvolio. Do you know what you say?   105

Maria. La you, and you speak ill of the devil, how he
takes it at heart. Pray God he be not bewitched.

Fabian. Carry his water to th' wise woman.°

Maria. Marry, and it shall be done tomorrow morning if I live. My lady would not lose him for more   110
than I'll say.

Malvolio. How now, mistress?

Maria. O Lord.

Toby. Prithee hold thy peace. This is not the way. Do
you not see you move° him? Let me alone with him.   115

Fabian. No way but gentleness; gently, gently. The
fiend is rough° and will not be roughly used.

Toby. Why, how now, my bawcock?° How dost thou,
chuck?°

Malvolio. Sir.   120

Toby. Ay, biddy, come with me. What, man, 'tis not

94 **How is't with you, man** (the Folio implausibly assigns this speech
to Fabian, but the contemptuous "man" suggests that the speaker
must be Malvolio's social superior)   96 **private** privacy   108 **Carry
his water to th' wise woman** i.e., for analysis   115 **move** agitate
117 **rough** violent   118 **bawcock** fine fellow (French *beau coq*)
119 **chuck** chick

for gravity to play at cherry-pit with Satan.° Hang
him, foul collier!°

Maria. Get him to say his prayers; good Sir Toby, get
125   him to pray.

Malvolio. My prayers, minx?

Maria. No, I warrant you, he will not hear of godli-
ness.

Malvolio. Go hang yourselves all! You are idle° shal-
130   low things; I am not of your element.° You shall
know more hereafter.   *Exit.*

Toby. Is't possible?

Fabian. If this were played upon a stage now, I could
condemn it as an improbable fiction.

135 *Toby.* His very genius° hath taken the infection of the
device, man.

Maria. Nay, pursue him now, lest the device take air
and taint.°

Fabian. Why, we shall make him mad indeed.

140 *Maria.* The house will be the quieter.

Toby. Come, we'll have him in a dark room and
bound. My niece is already in the belief that he's
mad. We may carry it° thus, for our pleasure and
his penance, till our very pastime, tired out of
145   breath, prompt us to have mercy on him; at which
time we will bring the device to the bar and crown
thee for a finder of madmen. But see, but see.

Enter Sir Andrew.

Fabian. More matter for a May morning.°

121–22 **'tis not for gravity . . . Satan** i.e., it is unsuitable for a man of
your dignity to play a children's game with Satan   123 **collier** vendor
of coals   129 **idle** trifling   130 **element** sphere   135 **genius** nature,
personality   137–138 **take air and taint** be exposed and spoiled
143 **carry it** i.e., go on with the joke   148 **More matter for a May
morning** i.e., another subject for a May-Day pageant

Andrew. Here's the challenge; read it. I warrant there's
    vinegar and pepper in't.   *150*

Fabian. Is't so saucy?°

Andrew. Ay, is't, I warrant him. Do but read.

Toby. Give me. [*Reads*] "Youth, whatsoever thou art,
    thou art but a scurvy fellow."

Fabian. Good, and valiant.   *155*

Toby. [*Reads*] "Wonder not nor admire° not in thy
    mind why I do call thee so, for I will show thee no
    reason for't."

Fabian. A good note that keeps you from the blow of
    the law.   *160*

Toby. [*Reads*] "Thou com'st to the Lady Olivia, and
    in my sight she uses thee kindly. But thou liest in
    thy throat; that is not the matter I challenge thee
    for."

Fabian. Very brief, and to exceeding good sense—   *165*
    less.

Toby. [*Reads*] "I will waylay thee going home; where
    if it be thy chance to kill me"—

Fabian. Good.

Toby. [*Reads*] "Thou kill'st me like a rogue and a   *170*
    villain."

Fabian. Still you keep o' th' windy side of the law.°
    Good.

Toby. [*Reads*] "Fare thee well, and God have mercy
    upon one of our souls. He may have mercy upon   *175*
    mine, but my hope is better, and so look to thyself.
    Thy friend, as thou usest him, and thy sworn enemy,
                    ANDREW AGUECHEEK."
    If this letter move him not, his legs cannot. I'll give't
    him.   *180*

151 **saucy** i.e., with "vinegar and pepper"   156 **admire** marvel
172 **o' th' windy side of the law** i.e., safe from prosecution

Maria. You may have very fit occasion for't. He is
now in some commerce° with my lady and will by
and by depart.

Toby. Go, Sir Andrew. Scout me for him at the corner
185   of the orchard like a bum-baily.° So soon as ever
thou seest him, draw; and as thou draw'st, swear
horrible; for it comes to pass oft that a terrible
oath, with a swaggering accent sharply twanged
off, gives manhood more approbation° than ever
190   proof° itself would have earned him. Away!

Andrew. Nay, let me alone for swearing.°   *Exit.*

Toby. Now will not I deliver his letter; for the behavior of the young gentleman gives him out to
be of good capacity and breeding; his employment
195   between his lord and my niece confirms no less.
Therefore this letter, being so excellently ignorant,
will breed no terror in the youth. He will find it
comes from a clodpoll.° But, sir, I will deliver his
challenge by word of mouth, set upon Aguecheek
200   a notable report of valor, and drive the gentleman
(as I know his youth will aptly receive it) into a
most hideous opinion of his rage, skill, fury, and
impetuosity. This will so fright them both that they
will kill one another by the look, like cockatrices.°

Enter Olivia and Viola.

205 *Fabian.* Here he comes with your niece. Give them
way till he take leave, and presently after him.°

Toby. I will meditate the while upon some horrid
message for a challenge.

[*Exeunt Sir Toby, Fabian, and Maria.*]
Olivia. I have said too much unto a heart of stone

---

182 **commerce** conversation   185 **bum-baily** bailiff, sheriff's officer
189 **approbation** attestation   190 **proof** actual trial   191 **let me
alone for swearing** i.e., do not worry about my ability at swearing
198 **clodpoll** dunce   204 **cockatrices** fabulous serpents that could
kill with a glance   205–206 **Give them way . . . after him** i.e., do
not interrupt them until he goes, and then follow him at once

And laid mine honor too unchary° on't.   210
There's something in me that reproves my fault;
But such a headstrong potent fault it is
That it but mocks reproof.

Viola. With the same havior° that your passion bears
Goes on my master's griefs.   215

Olivia. Here, wear this jewel° for me; 'tis my picture.
Refuse it not; it hath no tongue to vex you.
And I beseech you come again tomorrow.
What shall you ask of me that I'll deny,
That honor, saved, may upon asking give?   220

Viola. Nothing but this: your true love for my master.

Olivia. How with mine honor may I give him that
Which I have given to you?

Viola.   I will acquit you.

Olivia. Well, come again tomorrow. Fare thee well.
A fiend like thee° might bear my soul to hell.   225
                              [*Exit.*]

          Enter [*Sir*] *Toby and Fabian.*

Toby. Gentleman, God save thee.

Viola. And you, sir.

Toby. That defense thou hast, betake thee to't. Of
what nature the wrongs are thou hast done him,
I know not; but thy intercepter, full of despite,°   230
bloody as the hunter,° attends° thee at the orchard
end. Dismount thy tuck,° be yare° in thy preparation, for thy assailant is quick, skillful, and deadly.

Viola. You mistake, sir. I am sure no man hath any
quarrel to me. My remembrance is very free and   235
clear from any image of offense done to any man.

210 **unchary** carelessly   214 **havior** behavior   216 **jewel** i.e., jeweled
locket (?)   225 **like thee** i.e., with your attractions   230 **despite**
defiance   231 **bloody as the hunter** i.e., bloodthirsty as a hunting
dog   231 **attends** awaits   232 **Dismount thy tuck** unsheathe your
rapier   232 **yare** quick, prompt

Toby. You'll find it otherwise, I assure you. Therefore,
if you hold your life at any price, betake you to
your guard; for your opposite° hath in him what
240 youth, strength, skill, and wrath can furnish man
withal.°

Viola. I pray you, sir, what is he?

Toby. He is knight, dubbed with unhatched° rapier
and on carpet consideration,° but he is a devil in
245 private brawl. Souls and bodies hath he divorced
three; and his incensement at this moment is so im-
placable that satisfaction can be none but by pangs
of death and sepulcher. "Hob, nob"° is his word;
"give't or take't."

250 *Viola.* I will return again into the house and desire
some conduct° of the lady. I am no fighter. I have
heard of some kind of men that put quarrels pur-
posely on others to taste° their valor. Belike this
is a man of that quirk.

255 *Toby.* Sir, no. His indignation derives itself out of a
very competent° injury; therefore get you on and
give him his desire. Back you shall not to the
house, unless you undertake that with me which
with as much safety you might answer him. There-
260 fore on, or strip your sword stark naked; for
meddle° you must, that's certain, or forswear to
wear iron about you.

Viola. This is as uncivil as strange. I beseech you do
me this courteous office, as to know of the knight
265 what my offense to him is. It is something of my
negligence,° nothing of my purpose.

Toby. I will do so. Signior Fabian, stay you by this
gentleman till my return.   *Exit [Sir] Toby.*

Viola. Pray you, sir, do you know of this matter?

239 **opposite** adversary 241 **withal** with 243 **unhatched** unhacked
244 **on carpet consideration** i.e., not because of his exploits in the
field but through connections at court 248 **Hob, nob** have it, or
have it not 251 **conduct** escort 253 **taste** test 256 **competent**
sufficient 261 **meddle** engage him, fight 265–66 **of my negligence**
unintentional

Fabian. I know the knight is incensed against you, 270
even to a mortal arbitrament;° but nothing of the
circumstance more.

Viola. I beseech you, what manner of man is he?

Fabian. Nothing of that wonderful promise, to read
him by his form, as you are like to find him in the 275
proof of his valor. He is indeed, sir, the most skillful, bloody, and fatal opposite that you could pos-
sibly have found in any part of Illyria. Will you
walk towards him? I will make your peace with
him if I can. 280

Viola. I shall be much bound to you for't. I am one
that had rather go with sir priest than sir knight. I
care not who knows so much of my mettle.°

                              Exeunt.°

          Enter [Sir] Toby and [Sir] Andrew.

Toby. Why, man, he's a very devil; I have not seen
such a firago.° I had a pass° with him, rapier, scab- 285
bard, and all, and he gives me the stuck-in° with
such a mortal motion° that it is inevitable; and on
the answer° he pays you as surely as your feet hits
the ground they step on. They say he has been
fencer to the Sophy.° 290

Andrew. Pox on't, I'll not meddle with him.

Toby. Ay, but he will not now be pacified. Fabian
can scarce hold him yonder.

Andrew. Plague on't, and I thought he had been
valiant, and so cunning in fence,° I'd have seen 295

---

271 **mortal arbitrament** deadly trial   283 **mettle** character, disposition   283 s.d. **Exeunt** (this stage direction, which leaves the stage
empty, properly marks the ending of the scene, but the new scene
that opens with the entrance of Sir Toby and Sir Andrew is not
indicated as such in the Folio)   285 **firago** virago (probably a
phonetic spelling)   285 **pass** bout   286 **stuck-in** stoccado, thrust
287 **mortal motion** deadly pass   288 **answer** return   290 **Sophy**
Shah   295 **in fence** at fencing

him damned ere I'd have challenged him. Let him
let the matter slip, and I'll give him my horse,
gray Capilet.

Toby. I'll make the motion.° Stand here; make a good
300 show on't. This shall end without the perdition of
souls.° [*Aside*] Marry, I'll ride your horse as well
as I ride you.

Enter Fabian and Viola.

I have his horse to take up° the quarrel. I have
persuaded him the youth's a devil.

305 *Fabian.* He is as horribly conceited of him,° and pants
and looks pale, as if a bear were at his heels.

Toby. There's no remedy, sir; he will fight with you
for's oath° sake. Marry, he hath better bethought
him of his quarrel,° and he finds that now scarce
310 to be worth talking of. Therefore draw for the supportance of his vow.° He protests he will not hurt
you.

Viola. [*Aside*] Pray God defend me! A little thing
would make me tell them how much I lack of a
315 man.

Fabian. Give ground if you see him furious.

Toby. Come, Sir Andrew, there's no remedy. The
gentleman will for his honor's sake have one bout
with you; he cannot by the duello° avoid it; but he
320 has promised me, as he is a gentleman and a
soldier, he will not hurt you. Come on, to't.

Andrew. Pray God he keep his oath! [*Draws.*]

---

299 **motion** proposal   300–01 **perdition of souls** i.e., loss of life
303 **take up** settle   305 **He is as horribly conceited of him** i.e.,
Cesario has just as terrifying a notion of Sir Andrew   308 **oath**
oath's   309 **his quarrel** the cause of his resentment   310–11 **There-**
fore draw for the supportance of his vow i.e., make a show of valor
merely for the satisfaction of his oath   319 **duello** duelling code

Enter Antonio.

Viola. I do assure you 'tis against my will.   [*Draws.*]

Antonio. Put up your sword. If this young gentleman
   Have done offense, I take the fault on me;   325
   If you offend him, I for him defy you.

Toby. You, sir? Why, what are you?

Antonio. [*Draws*] One, sir, that for his love dares yet
   do more
   Than you have heard him brag to you he will.

Toby. Nay, if you be an undertaker,° I am for you.   330
                             [*Draws.*]

Enter Officers.

Fabian. O good Sir Toby, hold. Here come the officers.

Toby. [*To Antonio*] I'll be with you anon.

Viola. [*To Sir Andrew*] Pray, sir, put your sword up,
   if you please.

Andrew. Marry, will I, sir; and for that° I promised   335
   you, I'll be as good as my word. He will bear you
   easily, and reins well.

First Officer. This is the man; do thy office.°

Second Officer. Antonio, I arrest thee at the suit
   Of Count Orsino.

Antonio.   You do mistake me, sir.   340

First Officer. No, sir, no jot. I know your favor°
   well,
   Though now you have no sea-cap on your head.
   Take him away. He knows I know him well.

Antonio. I must obey. [*To Viola*] This comes with
   seeking you.

---

330 **an undertaker** one who takes up a challenge for another (with
perhaps a pun on "undertaker" as a government agent, i.e., scoun-
drel)   335 **for that** as for what (i.e., his horse, "gray Capilet")
338 **office** duty   341 **favor** face

345   But there's no remedy; I shall answer it.°
        What will you do, now my necessity
        Makes me to ask you for my purse? It grieves me
        Much more for what I cannot do for you
        Than what befalls myself. You stand amazed,
350   But be of comfort.

Second Officer. Come, sir, away.

Antonio. I must entreat of you some of that money.

Viola. What money, sir?
        For the fair kindness you have showed me here,
355   And part° being prompted by your present trouble,
        Out of my lean and low ability
        I'll lend you something. My having is not much.
        I'll make division of my present° with you.
        Hold, there's half my coffer.°

Antonio.   Will you deny me now?
360   Is't possible that my deserts to you
        Can lack persuasion?° Do not tempt my misery,
        Lest that it make me so unsound° a man
        As to upbraid you with those kindnesses
        That I have done for you.

Viola.   I know of none,
365   Nor know I you by voice or any feature.
        I hate ingratitude more in a man
        Than lying, vainness,° babbling, drunkenness,
        Or any taint of vice whose strong corruption
        Inhabits our frail blood.

Antonio.   O heavens themselves!

370 *Second Officer.* Come, sir, I pray you go.

Antonio. Let me speak a little. This youth that you
        see here
        I snatched one half out of the jaws of death;

345 **answer it** i.e., try to defend myself against the accusation
355 **part** partly   358 **present** present resources   359 **coffer** chest,
i.e., money   360–61 **deserts to you/Can lack persuasion** claims on
you can fail to be persuasive   362 **unsound** weak, unmanly
367 **vainness** (1) falseness (2) boasting

Relieved him with such sanctity of love,
And to his image, which methought did promise
Most venerable° worth, did I devotion.   375

First Officer. What's that to us? The time goes by.
Away.

Antonio. But, O, how vild° an idol proves this god!
Thou hast, Sebastian, done good feature° shame.
In nature there's no blemish but the mind;°
None can be called deformed but the unkind.°   380
Virtue is beauty; but the beauteous evil
Are empty trunks,° o'erflourished° by the devil.

First Officer. The man grows mad; away with him!
Come, come, sir.

Antonio. Lead me on.   *Exit [with Officers].*

Viola. Methinks his words do from such passion fly   385
That he believes himself; so do not I.
Prove true, imagination, O, prove true,
That I, dear brother, be now ta'en for you!

Toby. Come hither, knight; come hither, Fabian. We'll
whisper o'er a couplet or two of most sage saws.°   390

Viola. He named Sebastian. I my brother know
Yet living in my glass.° Even such and so
In favor was my brother, and he went
Still in this fashion, color, ornament,
For him I imitate. O, if it prove,   395
Tempests are kind, and salt waves fresh in love!
                              [*Exit.*]

Toby. A very dishonest° paltry boy, and more a
coward than a hare. His dishonesty appears in
leaving his friend here in necessity and denying
him; and for his cowardship, ask Fabian.   400

375 **venerable** worthy of veneration   377 **vild** vile   378 **feature**
shape, external appearance   379 **mind** (as distinguished from body
or "feature")   380 **unkind** unnatural   382 **trunks** chests   382 **o'er-
flourished** decorated with carving and painting   390 **sage saws** wise
maxims   392 **living in my glass** i.e., staring at me from my mirror
397 **dishonest** dishonorable

Fabian. A coward, a most devout coward; religious in it.°

Andrew. 'Slid,° I'll after him again and beat him.

Toby. Do; cuff him soundly, but never draw thy
405   sword.

Andrew. And I do not—   [*Exit.*]

Fabian. Come, let's see the event.°

Toby. I dare lay any money 'twill be nothing yet.°
                     Exit [*with Sir Andrew and Fabian*].

401–02 **religious in it** i.e., dedicated to his cowardice (following "devout")   403 **'Slid** by God's eyelid   407 **event** outcome   408 **yet** after all

ACT IV

Scene I. [*Before Olivia's house.*]

Enter Sebastian and Clown.

Clown. Will you make me believe that I am not sent
for you?

Sebastian. Go to, go to, thou art a foolish fellow. Let
me be clear of thee.

Clown. Well held out,° i' faith! No, I do not know   5
you; nor I am not sent to you by my lady, to bid
you come speak with her; nor your name is not
Master Cesario; nor this is not my nose neither.
Nothing that is so is so.

Sebastian. I prithee vent thy folly somewhere else.   10
Thou know'st not me.

Clown. Vent my folly! He has heard that word of
some great man, and now applies it to a fool. Vent
my folly! I am afraid this great lubber,° the world,
will prove a cockney.° I prithee now, ungird thy
strangeness,° and tell me what I shall vent° to my
lady. Shall I vent to her that thou art coming?

Sebastian. I prithee, foolish Greek,° depart from me.

IV.i.5 **held out** maintained   14 **lubber** lout   15 **cockney** affected
fop   15–16 **ungird thy strangeness** i.e., abandon your silly pretense
(of not recognizing me)   16 **vent** say   18 **Greek** buffoon

There's money for thee. If you tarry longer, I shall
20 give worse payment.

Clown. By my troth, thou hast an open hand. These
wise men that give fools money get themselves a
good report—after fourteen years' purchase.°

Enter [Sir] Andrew, [Sir] Toby, and Fabian.

Andrew. Now, sir, have I met you again? There's for
25 you!   [*Strikes Sebastian.*]

Sebastian. Why, there's for thee, and there, and there!
                              [*Strikes Sir Andrew.*]
Are all the people mad?

Toby. Hold, sir, or I'll throw your dagger o'er the
house.   [*Seizes Sebastian.*]

30 *Clown.* This will I tell my lady straight.° I would not
be in some of your coats for twopence.   [*Exit.*]

Toby. Come on, sir; hold.

Andrew. Nay, let him alone. I'll go another way to
work with him. I'll have an action of battery against
35 him,° if there be any law in Illyria. Though I
stroke° him first, yet it's no matter for that.

Sebastian. Let go thy hand.

Toby. Come, sir, I will not let you go. Come, my
young soldier, put up your iron. You are well
40 fleshed.° Come on.

Sebastian. I will be free from thee. [*Frees himself.*]
What wouldst thou now?
If thou dar'st tempt me further, draw thy sword.

Toby. What, what? Nay then, I must have an ounce
or two of this malapert° blood from you. [*Draws.*]

23 **after fourteen years' purchase** i.e., after a long delay, at a high
price   30 **straight** straightaway, at once   34–35 **have an action of
battery against him** charge him with assaulting me   36 **stroke**
struck   39–40 **well fleshed** i.e., made eager for fighting by having
tasted blood   44 **malapert** saucy

Enter Olivia.

Olivia. Hold, Toby! On thy life I charge thee hold!   45

Toby. Madam.

Olivia. Will it be ever thus? Ungracious wretch,
   Fit for the mountains and the barbarous caves,
   Where manners ne'er were preached! Out of my
     sight!
   Be not offended, dear Cesario.   50
   Rudesby,° begone.
       [*Exeunt Sir Toby, Sir Andrew, and Fabian.*]
               I prithee gentle friend,
   Let thy fair wisdom, not thy passion, sway°
   In this uncivil° and unjust extent°
   Against thy peace. Go with me to my house,
   And hear thou there how many fruitless pranks   55
   This ruffian hath botched up,° that thou thereby
   Mayst smile at this. Thou shalt not choose but go.
   Do not deny. Beshrew° his soul for me.
   He started° one poor heart° of mine, in thee.

Sebastian. What relish is in this?° How runs the
     stream?   60
   Or° I am mad, or else this is a dream.
   Let fancy still my sense in Lethe° steep;
   If it be thus to dream, still let me sleep!

Olivia. Nay, come, I prithee. Would thou'dst be ruled
     by me!

Sebastian. Madam, I will.

Olivia.   O, say so, and so be.   65
                    Exeunt.

---

51 **Rudesby** ruffian   52 **sway** rule   53 **uncivil** barbarous   53 **extent**
display   56 **botched up** clumsily contrived   58 **Beshrew** curse
59 **started** roused   59 **heart** (with a pun on "hart")   60 **What relish
is in this?** i.e., what does this mean?   61 **Or** either   62 **Lethe** in
classical mythology, the river of oblivion in Hades

Scene II. [*Olivia's house.*]

Enter Maria and Clown.

Maria. Nay, I prithee put on this gown and this beard;
make him believe thou art Sir Topas° the curate;
do it quickly. I'll call Sir Toby the whilst.° [*Exit.*]

Clown. Well, I'll put it on, and I will dissemble° my-
5 self in't, and I would I were the first that ever dissembled in such a gown. I am not tall enough to
become the function° well, nor lean enough to be
thought a good student;° but to be said an honest
man and a good housekeeper° goes as fairly as to
10 say a careful° man and a great scholar. The com-
petitors° enter.

Enter [Sir] Toby [and Maria].

Toby. Jove bless thee, Master Parson.

Clown. Bonos dies,° Sir Toby; for, as the old hermit
of Prague,° that never saw pen and ink, very wit-
15 tily said to a niece of King Gorboduc,° "That that
is"; so, I, being Master Parson, am Master Parson; for what is "that" but that, and "is" but is?

Toby. To him, Sir Topas.

Clown. What ho, I say. Peace in this prison!

20 *Toby.* The knave counterfeits well; a good knave.°

IV.ii.2 **Sir Topas** (the ridiculous hero of Chaucer's *Rime of Sir
Thopas,* a parody of chivalric romances)   3 **the whilst** meanwhile
4 **dissemble** disguise   7 **function** clerical office   8 **student** student
9 **good housekeeper** solid citizen   10 **careful** painstaking   10-11
competitors confederates   13 **Bonos dies** good day   13–14 **the old
hermit of Prague** (apparently the Clown's nonsensical invention)
15 **King Gorboduc** (a legendary king of Britain)   20 **knave** fellow

Malvolio within.

Malvolio. Who calls there?

Clown. Sir Topas the curate, who comes to visit Malvolio the lunatic.

Malvolio. Sir Topas, Sir Topas, good Sir Topas, go to my lady.   *25*

Clown. Out, hyperbolical° fiend! How vexest thou this man! Talkest thou nothing but of ladies?

Toby. Well said, Master Parson.

Malvolio. Sir Topas, never was man thus wronged. Good Sir Topas, do not think I am mad. They have   *30* laid me here in hideous darkness.

Clown. Fie, thou dishonest Satan. I call thee by the most modest° terms, for I am one of those gentle ones that will use the devil himself with courtesy. Say'st thou that house° is dark?   *35*

Malvolio. As hell, Sir Topas.

Clown. Why, it hath bay windows transparent as barricadoes,° and the clerestories° toward the south north are as lustrous as ebony; and yet complainest thou of obstruction?   *40*

Malvolio. I am not mad, Sir Topas. I say to you this house is dark.

Clown. Madman, thou errest. I say there is no darkness but ignorance, in which thou art more puzzled than the Egyptians in their fog.°   *45*

Malvolio. I say this house is as dark as ignorance, though ignorance were as dark as hell; and I say there was never man thus abused. I am no more

---

26 **hyperbolical** boisterous (a term from rhetoric meaning "exaggerated in style")   33 **most modest** mildest   35 **house** madman's cell   37-38 **barricadoes** barricades   38 **clerestories** upper windows   45 **Egyptians in their fog** (to plague the Egyptians Moses brought a "thick darkness" that lasted three days; see Exodus 10:21-23)

mad than you are. Make the trial of it in any con-
50 stant question.°

Clown. What is the opinion of Pythagoras° concerning
wild fowl?

Malvolio. That the soul of our grandam might hap-
pily° inhabit a bird.

55 *Clown.* What think'st thou of his opinion?

Malvolio. I think nobly of the soul and no way approve
his opinion.

Clown. Fare thee well. Remain thou still in darkness.
Thou shalt hold th' opinion of Pythagoras ere I
60 will allow of thy wits,° and fear to kill a woodcock,° lest thou dispossess the soul of thy grandam.
Fare thee well.

Malvolio. Sir Topas, Sir Topas!

Toby. My most exquisite Sir Topas!

65 *Clown.* Nay, I am for all waters.°

Maria. Thou mightst have done this without thy beard
and gown. He sees thee not.

Toby. To him in thine own voice, and bring me word
how thou find'st him. [*To Maria*] I would we were
70 well rid of this knavery. If he may be conveniently
delivered,° I would he were; for I am now so far
in offense with my niece that I cannot pursue with
any safety this sport to the upshot.° [*To the Clown*]
Come by and by to my chamber. *Exit* [*with Maria*].

75 *Clown.* [*Sings*] "Hey, Robin, jolly Robin,
            Tell me how thy lady does."°

49–50 **constant question** consistent topic, normal conversation
51 **Pythagoras** (ancient Greek philosopher who expounded the doctrine of the transmigration of souls)   53–54 **happily** haply, perhaps
60 **allow of thy wits** acknowledge your sanity   60–61 **woodcock** (a
proverbially stupid bird)   65 **I am for all waters** i.e., I can turn my
hand to any trade   71 **delivered** released   73 **upshot** conclusion
75–76 **Hey, Robin . . . lady does** (the Clown sings an old ballad)

Malvolio. Fool.

Clown. "My lady is unkind, perdie."°

Malvolio. Fool.

Clown. "Alas, why is she so?"　　　　　　　　　　　*80*

Malvolio. Fool, I say.

Clown. "She loves another." Who calls, ha?

Malvolio. Good fool, as ever thou wilt deserve well at my hand, help me to a candle, and pen, ink, and paper. As I am a gentleman, I will live to be thank-　*85* ful to thee for't.

Clown. Master Malvolio?

Malvolio. Ay, good fool.

Clown. Alas, sir, how fell you besides your five wits?°

Malvolio. Fool, there was never man so notoriously°　*90* abused. I am as well in my wits, fool, as thou art.

Clown. But as well? Then you are mad indeed, if you be no better in your wits than a fool.

Malvolio. They have here propertied° me; keep me in darkness, send ministers to me, asses, and do all　*95* they can to face me out of my wits.°

Clown. Advise you° what you say. The minister is here.°— Malvolio, Malvolio, thy wits the heavens restore. Endeavor thyself to sleep and leave thy vain bibble babble.　　　　　　　　　　　　　　　*100*

Malvolio. Sir Topas.

Clown. Maintain no words with him, good fellow.

---

78 **perdie** certainly　89 **how fell you besides your five wits?** i.e., how did you happen to become mad?　90 **notoriously** outrageously 94 **propertied** i.e., used me as a mere object, not a human being 96 **face me out of my wits** i.e., impudently insist that I am mad 97 **Advise you** consider carefully　97–98 **The minister is here** (for the next few lines the Clown uses two voices, his own and that of Sir Topas)

—Who, I, sir? Not I, sir. God buy you,° good Sir
Topas.—Marry, amen.—I will, sir, I will.

105 *Malvolio*. Fool, fool, fool, I say!

Clown. Alas, sir, be patient. What say you, sir? I am
shent° for speaking to you.

Malvolio. Good fool, help me to some light and some
paper. I tell thee, I am as well in my wits as any
110   man in Illyria.

Clown. Well-a-day that you were,° sir.

Malvolio. By this hand, I am. Good fool, some ink,
paper, and light; and convey what I will set down
to my lady. It shall advantage thee more than ever
115   the bearing of letter did.

Clown. I will help you to't. But tell me true, are you
not mad indeed, or do you but counterfeit?°

Malvolio. Believe me, I am not. I tell thee true.

Clown. Nay, I'll ne'er believe a madman till I see his
120   brains. I will fetch you light and paper and ink.

Malvolio. Fool, I'll requite it in the highest degree. I
prithee be gone.

Clown. [*Sings*]   I am gone, sir.
                         And anon, sir,
125   I'll be with you again,
                            In a trice,
                            Like to the old Vice,°
                     Your need to sustain.°
                   Who with dagger of lath,
130   In his rage and his wrath,
                         Cries "Ah ha" to the devil.
                      Like a mad lad,

---

103 **God buy you** God be with you, i.e., good-bye   107 **shent** re-
buked   111 **Well-a-day that you were** alas, if only you were   117
counterfeit pretend   127 **Vice** (in the morality plays, a stock mischievous character who usually carried a wooden dagger)   128 **Your
need to sustain** i.e., in order to help you resist the Devil

"Pare thy nails, dad."
            Adieu, goodman devil.°   *Exit.*

Scene III. [*Olivia's garden.*]

Enter Sebastian.

Sebastian. This is the air; that is the glorious sun;
    This pearl she gave me, I do feel't and see't;
    And though 'tis wonder that enwraps me thus,
    Yet 'tis not madness. Where's Antonio then?
    I could not find him at the Elephant;   5
    Yet there he was,° and there I found this credit,°
    That he did range the town to seek me out.
    His counsel now might do me golden service;
    For though my soul disputes well with my sense°
    That this may be some error, but no madness,   10
    Yet doth this accident and flood of fortune
    So far exceed all instance,° all discourse,°
    That I am ready to distrust mine eyes
    And wrangle with my reason that persuades me
    To any other trust° but that I am mad,   15
    Or else the lady's mad. Yet, if 'twere so,
    She could not sway° her house, command her
        followers,
    Take and give back affairs and their dispatch°
    With such a smooth, discreet, and stable bearing
    As I perceive she does. There's something in't   20
    That is deceivable.° But here the lady comes.

---

134 **Adieu, goodman devil** (a much emended line; "goodman" [Folio
"good man"], a title for a yeoman or any man of substance not of
gentle birth, roughly corresponds to our "mister")   IV.iii.6 **was had**
been   6 **credit** belief   9 **my soul disputes well with my sense** my
reason agrees with the evidence of my senses   12 **instance** precedent
12 **discourse** reason   15 **trust** belief   17 **sway** rule   18 **Take and
give . . . their dispatch** i.e., assume and discharge the management of
affairs   21 **deceivable** deceptive

Enter Olivia and Priest.

Olivia. Blame not this haste of mine. If you mean well,
     Now go with me and with this holy man
     Into the chantry by.° There, before him,
25   And underneath that consecrated roof,
     Plight me the full assurance of your faith,
     That my most jealious° and too doubtful soul
     May live at peace. He shall conceal it
     Whiles° you are willing it shall come to note,°
30   What time we will our celebration keep°
     According to my birth. What do you say?

Sebastian. I'll follow this good man and go with you
     And having sworn truth, ever will be true.

Olivia. Then lead the way, good father, and heavens
          so shine
35   That they may fairly note° this act of mine.
                                              Exeunt.

24 **chantry by** nearby chapel   27 **jealious** jealous, anxious   29 **Whiles**
until   29 **come to note** be made public   30 **our celebration keep**
celebrate our marriage ceremony (as distinguished from the formal
compact of betrothal)   35 **fairly note** look with favor on

ACT V

Scene I. [*Before Olivia's house.*]

Enter Clown and Fabian.

Fabian. Now as thou lov'st me, let me see his° letter.

Clown. Good Master Fabian, grant me another request.

Fabian. Anything.

Clown. Do not desire to see this letter. 5

Fabian. This is to give a dog, and in recompense desire my dog again.

Enter Duke, Viola, Curio, and Lords.

Duke. Belong you to the Lady Olivia, friends?

Clown. Ay, sir, we are some of her trappings.

Duke. I know thee well. How dost thou, my good 10
fellow?

Clown. Truly, sir, the better for my foes, and the worse for my friends.

V.i.1 **his** i.e., Malvolio's

Duke. Just the contrary: the better for thy friends.

15 *Clown.* No, sir, the worse.

Duke. How can that be?

Clown. Marry, sir, they praise me and make an ass of
me. Now my foes tell me plainly I am an ass; so
that by my foes, sir, I profit in the knowledge of
20 myself, and by my friends I am abused;° so that,
conclusions to be as kisses,° if your four negatives°
make your two affirmatives,° why then, the worse
for my friends, and the better for my foes.

Duke. Why, this is excellent.

25 *Clown.* By my troth, sir, no, though it please you to
be one of my friends.

Duke. Thou shalt not be the worse for me. There's
gold.

Clown. But that it would be double-dealing,° sir, I
30 would you could make it another.

Duke. O, you give me ill counsel.

Clown. Put your grace° in your pocket, sir, for this
once, and let your flesh and blood obey it.

Duke. Well, I will be so much a sinner to be a double-
35 dealer. There's another.°

Clown. Primo, secundo, tertio° is a good play;° and
the old saying is "The third pays for all." The
triplex,° sir, is a good tripping measure; or the
bells of Saint Bennet,° sir, may put you in mind—
40 one, two, three.

Duke. You can fool no more money out of me at this

---

20 **abused** deceived   21 **conclusions to be as kisses** i.e., if conclusions
may be compared to kisses (when a coy girl's repeated denials really
mean assent)   21 **negatives** i.e., lips (?)   22 **affirmatives** i.e., mouths
(?)   29 **double-dealing** (1) giving twice (2) duplicity   32 **grace** (1)
title of nobility (2) generosity   35 **another** i.e., coin   36 **Primo,
secundo, tertio** one, two, three   36 **play** child's game (?)   38 **triplex**
triple time in dancing   39 **Saint Bennet** St. Benedict (a church)

throw.° If you will let your lady know I am here
to speak with her, and bring her along with you, it
may awake my bounty further.

Clown. Marry, sir, lullaby to your bounty till I come   45
again. I go, sir; but I would not have you to think
that my desire of having is the sin of covetousness.
But, as you say, sir, let your bounty take a nap; I
will awake it anon.   *Exit.*

Enter Antonio and Officers.

Viola. Here comes the man, sir, that did rescue me.   50

Duke. That face of his I do remember well;
    Yet when I saw it last, it was besmeared
    As black as Vulcan° in the smoke of war.
    A baubling° vessel was he captain of,
    For shallow draught and bulk unprizable,°   55
    With which such scathful° grapple did he make
    With the most noble bottom° of our fleet
    That very envy and the tongue of loss°
    Cried fame and honor on him. What's the matter?

First Officer. Orsino, this is that Antonio   60
    That took the *Phoenix* and her fraught° from
        Candy;°
    And this is he that did the *Tiger* board
    When your young nephew Titus lost his leg.
    Here in the streets, desperate of shame and state,°
    In private brabble° did we apprehend him.   65

Viola. He did me kindness, sir; drew on my side;°
    But in conclusion put strange speech upon me.°
    I know not what 'twas but distraction.°

42 **throw** throw of the dice   53 **Vulcan** Roman god of fire and
patron of blacksmiths   54 **baubling** insignificant   55 **For shallow
draught and bulk unprizable** i.e., virtually worthless on account of
its small size   56 **scathful** destructive   57 **bottom** ship   58 **very
envy and the tongue of loss** even enmity and the voice of the losers
61 **fraught** freight, cargo   61 **Candy** Candia, Crete   64 **desperate
of shame and state** i.e., recklessly disregarding his shameful past
behavior and the requirements of public order   65 **brabble** brawl
66 **drew on my side** i.e., drew his sword in my defense   67 **put
strange speech upon me** spoke to me so oddly   68 **distraction** madness

Duke. Notable° pirate, thou salt-water thief,
70   What foolish boldness brought thee to their mercies
       Whom thou in terms so bloody and so dear°
       Hast made thine enemies?

Antonio.   Orsino, noble sir,
       Be pleased that I shake off these names you give me.
       Antonio never yet was thief or pirate,
75   Though I confess, on base and ground enough,
       Orsino's enemy. A witchcraft drew me hither.
       That most ingrateful boy there by your side
       From the rude sea's enraged and foamy mouth
       Did I redeem. A wrack° past hope he was.
80   His life I gave him, and did thereto add
       My love without retention or restraint,
       All his in dedication. For his sake
       Did I expose myself (pure° for his love)
       Into the danger of this adverse° town;
85   Drew to defend him when he was beset;
       Where being apprehended, his false cunning
       (Not meaning to partake with me in danger)
       Taught him to face me out of his acquaintance,°
       And grew a twenty years removèd thing
90   While one would wink; denied me mine own purse,
       Which I had recommended° to his use
       Not half an hour before.

Viola.   How can this be?

Duke. When came he to this town?

Antonio. Today, my lord; and for three months before,
95   No int'rim, not a minute's vacancy,
       Both day and night did we keep company.

                Enter Olivia and Attendants.

Duke. Here comes the Countess; now heaven walks on
       earth.

---

69 **Notable** notorious   71 **dear** grievous   79 **wrack** wreck   83 **pure**
purely   84 **adverse** unfriendly   88 **to face me out of his acquaintance** i.e., brazenly to deny any knowledge of me   91 **recommended**
given

But for° thee, fellow: fellow, thy words are mad-
ness.
Three months this youth hath tended upon me;
But more of that anon. Take him aside.   100

Olivia. What would my lord, but that° he may not
have,
Wherein Olivia may seem serviceable?
Cesario, you do not keep promise with me.

Viola. Madam?

Duke. Gracious Olivia—   105

Olivia. What do you say, Cesario?—Good my lord°—

Viola. My lord would speak; my duty hushes me.

Olivia. If it be aught to the old tune, my lord,
It is as fat and fulsome° to mine ear
As howling after music.

Duke.   Still so cruel?   110

Olivia. Still so constant, lord.

Duke. What, to perverseness? You uncivil lady,
To whose ingrate and unauspicious° altars
My soul the faithfull'st off'rings have breathed out
That e'er devotion tendered. What shall I do?   115

Olivia. Even what it please my lord, that shall become
him.

Duke. Why should I not, had I the heart to do it,
Like to th' Egyptian thief° at point of death,
Kill what I love?—a savage jealousy
That sometime savors nobly. But hear me this: 120
Since you to non-regardance° cast my faith,

98 **But for** as for   101 **but that** except that which (i.e., my love)
106 **Good my lord** i.e., please be silent (so Cesario may speak)
109 **fat and fulsome** gross and repulsive   113 **ingrate and unauspi-
cious** ungrateful and unpropitious   118 **th' Egyptian thief** (in Heli-
odorus' *Ethiopica*, a Greek romance translated by Thomas Under-
down about 1569, the bandit Thyamis, besieged in a cave, plans to
kill the captive princess Clariclea, the object of his hopeless love;
but in the darkness he kills another woman instead)   121 **non-
regardance** neglect

And that° I partly know the instrument
That screws° me from my true place in your favor,
Live you the marble-breasted tyrant still.
125 But this your minion, whom I know you love,
And whom, by heaven I swear, I tender° dearly,
Him will I tear out of that cruel eye
Where he sits crownèd in his master's spite.
Come, boy, with me. My thoughts are ripe in
     mischief.
130 I'll sacrifice the lamb that I do love
To spite a raven's heart within a dove.   [*Going.*]

Viola. And I, most jocund, apt,° and willingly,
To do you rest° a thousand deaths would die.
                                        [*Following.*]

Olivia. Where goes Cesario?

Viola.   After him I love
135 More than I love these eyes, more than my life,
More, by all mores,° than e'er I shall love wife.
If I do feign, you witnesses above
Punish my life for tainting of my love!

Olivia. Ay me detested, how am I beguiled!

Viola. Who does beguile you? Who does do you
140   wrong?

Olivia. Hast thou forgot thyself? Is it so long?
Call forth the holy father.   [*Exit an Attendant.*]

Duke.   [*To Viola*] Come, away!

Olivia. Whither, my lord? Cesario, husband, stay.

Duke. Husband?

Olivia.   Ay, husband. Can he that deny?

Duke. Her husband, sirrah?°

145 *Viola.*   No, my lord, not I.

___

122 **that** since   123 **screws** forces   126 **tender** hold   132 **apt** readily
133 **do you rest** give you peace   136 **mores** i.e., possible comparisons
144 **sirrah** (customary form of address to a menial)

Olivia. Alas, it is the baseness of thy fear
 That makes thee strangle thy propriety.°
 Fear not, Cesario; take thy fortunes up;
 Be that thou know'st thou art, and then thou art
 As great as that° thou fear'st.

Enter Priest.

                              O, welcome, father!   *150*
 Father, I charge thee by thy reverence
 Here to unfold—though lately we intended
 To keep in darkness what occasion now
 Reveals before 'tis ripe—what thou dost know
 Hath newly passed between this youth and me.   *155*

Priest. A contract° of eternal bond of love,
 Confirmed by mutual joinder of your hands,
 Attested by the holy close of lips,
 Strength'ned by interchangement of your rings;
 And all the ceremony of this compact°   *160*
 Sealed in my function,° by my testimony;
 Since when, my watch hath told me, toward my
        grave
 I have traveled but two hours.

Duke. O thou dissembling cub, what wilt thou be
 When time hath sowed a grizzle on thy case?°   *165*
 Or will not else thy craft° so quickly grow
 That thine own trip° shall be thine overthrow?
 Farewell, and take her; but direct thy feet
 Where thou and I, henceforth, may never meet.

Viola. My lord, I do protest.

Olivia.   O, do not swear.   *170*
 Hold little° faith, though thou hast too much fear.

Enter Sir Andrew.

147 **strangle thy propriety** deny your identity   150 **that** him who
(i.e., the Duke)   156 **contract** betrothal   160 **compact** (accent on
second syllable)   161 **Sealed in my function** i.e., ratified by me in
my priestly office   165 **a grizzle on thy case** gray hairs on your skin
166 **craft** duplicity   167 **trip** craftiness   171 **little** i.e., at least a little

Andrew. For the love of God, a surgeon! Send one
presently° to Sir Toby.

Olivia. What's the matter?

175 *Andrew.* H'as° broke my head across, and has given
Sir Toby a bloody coxcomb° too. For the love of
God, your help! I had rather than forty pound I
were at home.

Olivia. Who has done this, Sir Andrew?

180 *Andrew.* The Count's gentleman, one Cesario. We
took him for a coward, but he's the very devil
incardinate.°

Duke. My gentleman Cesario?

Andrew. Od's lifelings,° here he is! You broke my
185 head for nothing; and that that I did, I was set on
to do't by Sir Toby.

Viola. Why do you speak to me? I never hurt you.
You drew your sword upon me without cause,
But I bespake you fair° and hurt you not.

Enter [Sir] Toby and Clown.

190 *Andrew.* If a bloody coxcomb be a hurt, you have
hurt me. I think you set nothing by a bloody coxcomb. Here comes Sir Toby halting;° you shall hear
more. But if he had not been in drink, he would
have tickled you othergates° than he did.

195 *Duke.* How now, gentleman? How is't with you?

Toby. That's all one! Has hurt me, and there's th'
end on't. Sot,° didst see Dick Surgeon, sot?

Clown. O, he's drunk, Sir Toby, an hour agone. His
eyes were set° at eight i' th' morning.

173 **presently** immediately   175 **H'as** he has   176 **coxcomb** pate
182 **incardinate** incarnate   184 **Od's lifelings** by God's life   189 **bespake you fair** addressed you courteously   192 **halting** limping
194 **othergates** otherwise   197 **Sot** fool   199 **set** closed

Toby. Then he's a rogue and a passy measures   200
pavin.° I hate a drunken rogue.

Olivia. Away with him! Who hath made this havoc
with them?

Andrew. I'll help you, Sir Toby, because we'll be
dressed° together.   205

Toby. Will you help—an ass-head and a coxcomb
and a knave, a thin-faced knave, a gull?

Olivia. Get him to bed, and let his hurt be looked to.
[*Exeunt Clown, Fabian, Sir Toby,
and Sir Andrew.*]

Enter Sebastian.

Sebastian. I am sorry, madam, I have hurt your
kinsman;
But had it been the brother of my blood,   210
I must have done no less with wit and safety.°
You throw a strange regard° upon me, and by that
I do perceive it hath offended you.
Pardon me, sweet one, even for the vows
We made each other but so late ago.   215

Duke. One face, one voice, one habit,° and two
persons—
A natural perspective° that is and is not.

Sebastian. Antonio, O my dear Antonio,
How have the hours racked and tortured me
Since I have lost thee!   220

Antonio. Sebastian are you?

Sebastian.   Fear'st thou° that, Antonio?

200–01 **passy measures pavin** i.e., *passamezzo* pavan, a slow and
stately dance of eight bars (hence its relevance to the surgeon whose
eyes had "set at eight")   204–05 **be dressed** have our wounds dressed
211 **with wit and safety** i.e., with a sensible regard for my safety
212 **strange regard** unfriendly look   216 **habit** costume   217 **A
natural perspective** i.e., a natural optical illusion (like that produced
by a stereoscope, which converts two images into one)   221 **Fear'st
thou** do you doubt

Antonio. How have you made division of yourself?
  An apple cleft in two is not more twin
  Than these two creatures. Which is Sebastian?

225 *Olivia.* Most wonderful.

Sebastian. Do I stand there? I never had a brother;
  Nor can there be that deity in my nature
  Of here and everywhere.° I had a sister,
  Whom the blind waves and surges have devoured.
230   Of charity,° what kin are you to me?
  What countryman? What name? What parentage?

Viola. Of Messaline; Sebastian was my father;
  Such a Sebastian was my brother too;
  So went he suited° to his watery tomb.
235   If spirits can assume both form and suit,°
  You come to fright us.

Sebastian.   A spirit I am indeed,
  But am in that dimension grossly clad
  Which from the womb I did participate.°
  Were you a woman, as the rest goes even,°
240   I should my tears let fall upon your cheek
  And say, "Thrice welcome, drownèd Viola!"

Viola. My father had a mole upon his brow.

Sebastian. And so had mine.

Viola. And died that day when Viola from her birth
245   Had numb'red thirteen years.

Sebastian. O, that record° is lively in my soul!
  He finishèd indeed his mortal act
  That day that made my sister thirteen years.

Viola. If nothing lets° to make us happy both
250   But this my masculine usurped attire,

227–28 **Nor can there be ... everywhere** i.e., nor can I, like God, be
everywhere at once 230 **Of charity** out of simple kindness 234
suited clothed 235 **form and suit** body and clothing 237–38 **am
in that dimension ... participate** i.e., clothed in the bodily form that,
like other mortals, I acquired at birth 239 **as the rest goes even** i.e.,
as other circumstances seem to indicate 246 **record** history (accent
on second syllable) 249 **lets** interferes

Do not embrace me till each circumstance
Of place, time, fortune do cohere and jump°
That I am Viola; which to confirm,
I'll bring you to a captain in this town,
Where lie my maiden weeds;° by whose gentle help   255
I was preserved to serve this noble Count.
All the occurrence of my fortune since
Hath been between this lady and this lord.

Sebastian. [*To Olivia*] So comes it, lady, you have
    been mistook.
But nature to her bias drew° in that.   260
You would have been contracted to a maid;
Nor are you therein, by my life, deceived:
You are betrothed both to a maid and man.

Duke. Be not amazed; right noble is his blood.
If this be so, as yet the glass° seems true,   265
I shall have share in this most happy wrack.
[*To Viola*] Boy, thou hast said to me a thousand
    times
Thou never shouldst love woman like to me.

Viola. And all those sayings will I over° swear,
And all those swearings keep as true in soul   270
As doth that orbèd continent° the fire
That severs day from night.

Duke.   Give me thy hand,
And let me see thee in thy woman's weeds.

Viola. The captain that did bring me first on shore
Hath my maid's garments. He upon some action   275
Is now in durance, at Malvolio's suit,°
A gentleman, and follower of my lady's.

Olivia. He shall enlarge° him. Fetch Malvolio hither.

252 **cohere and jump** i.e., fall together and agree   255 **weeds** clothes
260 **nature to her bias drew** i.e., nature followed her normal inclination   265 **glass** i.e., the "natural perspective" of line 217   269 **over**
repeatedly   271 **orbèd continent** in Ptolemaic astronomy, the sphere
of the sun   275–76 **He upon some action . . . Malvolio's suit** i.e.,
at Malvolio's instigation he is now imprisoned upon some legal
charge   278 **enlarge** release

And yet alas, now I remember me,
280 They say, poor gentleman, he's much distract.

Enter Clown with a letter, and Fabian.

A most extracting° frenzy of mine own
From my remembrance clearly banished his.
How does he, sirrah?

Clown. Truly, madam, he holds Belzebub at the
285 stave's end° as well as a man in his case° may do.
Has here writ a letter to you; I should have given't
you today morning. But as a madman's epistles are
no gospels, so it skills° not much when they are
delivered.

290 *Olivia.* Open't and read it.

Clown. Look then to be well edified, when the fool
delivers the madman. [*Reads in a loud voice*] "By
the Lord, madam"—

Olivia. How now? Art thou mad?

295 *Clown.* No, madam, I do but read madness. And your
ladyship will have it as it ought to be, you must
allow *vox.*°

Olivia. Prithee read i' thy right wits.

Clown. So I do, madonna; but to read his right wits is
300 to read thus. Therefore perpend,° my princess, and
give ear.

Olivia. [*To Fabian*] Read it you, sirrah.

Fabian. (*Reads*) "By the Lord, madam, you wrong
me, and the world shall know it. Though you have
305 put me into darkness, and given your drunken
cousin rule over me, yet have I the benefit of my
senses as well as your ladyship. I have your own
letter that induced me to the semblance I put on;

281 **extracting** i.e., obliterating (in that it draws me from all thoughts
of Malvolio's "frenzy")   284–85 **he holds Belzebub at the stave's
end** i.e., he keeps the fiend at a distance   285 **case** condition
288 **skills** matters   297 **vox** i.e., an appropriately loud voice   300
perpend pay attention

with the which I doubt not but to do myself much
right, or you much shame. Think of me as you　310
please. I leave my duty a little unthought of, and
speak out of my injury.
　　　　　　　THE MADLY USED MALVOLIO."

Olivia. Did he write this?

Clown. Ay, madam.　　　　　　　　　　　　　315

Duke. This savors not much of distraction.

Olivia. See him delivered, Fabian; bring him hither.
　　　　　　　　　　　　　　　[Exit Fabian.]
　My lord, so please you, these things further thought
　　on,
　To think me as well a sister as a wife,
　One day shall crown th' alliance on't, so please you,　320
　Here at my house and at my proper° cost.

Duke. Madam, I am most apt° t' embrace your offer.
　[To Viola] Your master quits° you; and for your
　　service done him,
　So much against the mettle of your sex,
　So far beneath your soft and tender breeding,　325
　And since you called me master for so long,
　Here is my hand; you shall from this time be
　Your master's mistress.

Olivia.　　　　　　A sister; you are she.

　　　　　Enter *[Fabian, with]* Malvolio.

Duke. Is this the madman?

Olivia.　　　　　　Ay, my lord, this same.
　How now, Malvolio?

Malvolio.　　　　　Madam, you have done me wrong,　330
　Notorious° wrong.

Olivia.　　　　　Have I, Malvolio? No.

Malvolio. Lady, you have. Pray you peruse that letter.
　You must not now deny it is your hand.

321 **proper** own　322 **apt** ready　323 **quits** releases　331 **Notorious**
notable

Write from it° if you can, in hand or phrase,
335 Or say 'tis not your seal, not your invention.°
You can say none of this. Well, grant it then,
And tell me, in the modesty of honor,°
Why you have given me such clear lights of favor,
Bade me come smiling and cross-gartered to you,
340 To put on yellow stockings, and to frown
Upon Sir Toby and the lighter° people;
And, acting this in an obedient hope,
Why have you suffered me to be imprisoned,
Kept in a dark house, visited by the priest,
345 And made the most notorious geck and gull°
That e'er invention played on? Tell me why.

Olivia. Alas, Malvolio, this is not my writing,
Though I confess much like the character;
But, out of° question, 'tis Maria's hand.
350 And now I do bethink me, it was she
First told me thou wast mad; then cam'st in smiling,
And in such forms which here were presupposed°
Upon thee in the letter. Prithee be content.
This practice hath most shrewdly passed° upon thee;
355 But when we know the grounds and authors of it,
Thou shalt be both the plaintiff and the judge
Of thine own cause.

Fabian.   Good madam, hear me speak,
And let no quarrel, nor no brawl to come,
Taint the condition of this present hour,
360 Which I have wond'red at. In hope it shall not,
Most freely I confess myself and Toby
Set this device against Malvolio here,
Upon some stubborn and uncourteous parts°
We had conceived against him. Maria writ
365 The letter, at Sir Toby's great importance,°

334 **from it** differently   335 **invention** composition   336 **in the
modesty of honor** i.e., with a proper regard to your own honor
341 **lighter** lesser   345 **geck and gull** fool and dupe   349 **out of**
beyond   352 **presupposed** imposed   354 **This practice hath most
shrewdly passed** i.e., this trick has most mischievously worked   363
Upon some stubborn and uncourteous parts i.e., because of some
unyielding and discourteous traits of character   365 **importance** importunity

In recompense whereof he hath married her.
How with a sportful malice it was followed
May rather pluck on° laughter than revenge,
If that° the injuries be justly weighed
That have on both sides passed.   *370*

Olivia. Alas, poor fool,° how have they baffled° thee!

Clown. Why, "some are born great, some achieve
greatness, and some have greatness thrown upon
them." I was one, sir, in this interlude,° one Sir
Topas, sir; but that's all one. "By the Lord, fool, I   *375*
am not mad!" But do you remember, "Madam, why
laugh you at such a barren rascal? And you smile
not, he's gagged"? And thus the whirligig of tin..
brings in his revenges.

Malvolio. I'll be revenged on the whole pack of you!   *380*
                                                    [*Exit.*]

Olivia. He hath been most notoriously abused.

Duke. Pursue him and entreat him to a peace.
He hath not told us of the captain yet.
When that is known, and golden time convents,°
A solemn combination shall be made   *385*
Of our dear souls. Meantime, sweet sister,
We will not part from hence. Cesario, come—
For so you shall be while you are a man,
But when in other habits you are seen,
Orsino's mistress and his fancy's° queen.   *390*
                          Exeunt [*all but the Clown*].

                    Clown sings.°

When that I was and a° little tiny boy,
    With hey, ho, the wind and the rain,
A foolish thing was but a toy,°

368 **pluck on** prompt   369 **If that** if   371 **fool** (here, a term of affection and compassion)   371 **baffled** publicly humiliated   374 **interlude** little play   384 **convents** is suitable (?)   390 **fancy's** love's
s.d. **Clown sings** (since no source has been found for the Clown's
song—which certain editors have inexplicably denounced as dog-
gerel—we may assume that it is Shakespeare's)   391 **and a** a
393 **toy** trifle

For the rain it raineth every day.

395   But when I came to man's estate,
          With hey, ho, the wind and the rain,
        'Gainst knaves and thieves men shut their gate,
          For the rain it raineth every day.

        But when I came, alas, to wive,
400   With hey, ho, the wind and the rain,
        By swaggering could I never thrive,
          For the rain it raineth every day.

        But when I came unto my beds,
          With hey, ho, the wind and the rain,
405   With tosspots° still had drunken heads,
          For the rain it raineth every day.

        A great while ago the world begun,
          Hey, ho, the wind and the rain;
        But that's all one, our play is done,
410   And we'll strive to please you every day.
                                              [*Exit.*]

                      FINIS.

---

405 **tosspots** sots

Textual Note

The text of *Twelfth Night,* for which the sole source is the Folio of 1623, is, if not immaculate, so clean and tidy that it presents almost no problems. Apparently set up from the prompt copy or a transcript of it, the Folio of course contains a few misprints (like *incardinatc* for *incardinate* at V.i.182), a few presumed or obvious errors in speech-headings (like those at II.v.34, 38, where Sir Toby is perhaps confused with Fabian, or at III.iv.24, where Malvolio is assigned a speech that clearly is not his), and a few lines (for example, II.ii.12 and III.iii.15) that seem to need some sort of emendation. Moreover, the fact that the Clown is given all the lovely songs that were perhaps originally Viola's (as suggested at I.ii.57–59 and II.iv.42–43) has been cited as a token of revision. In general, however, the text, as all its editors have gratefully conceded, is one of almost unexampled purity.

In the present edition, therefore, it is followed very closely, even in such forms as *studient, jealious, wrack* (for *wreck*) and *vild,* which preserve, we may suppose, not only Shakespeare's spelling but also his pronunciation. But *prethee, divil, murther, Sathan* (for *Satan*), *Anthonio,* and *berd* (which occurs once for *beard*) are given in modern spelling. A few emendations sanctioned by long and universal approbation—like Pope's *Arion* for *Orion* at I.ii.15, Theobald's inspired *curl by* for *coole my* at I.iii.96, and Hanmer's *staniel* for *stallion* at II.v.115— have been admitted here, as have one or two superior readings from the later Folios (for example, *tang* for *langer* at III.iv.73). However, such attractive but unnecessary emendations as Pope's *south* for *sound* at I.i.5 have been rejected, and the few real cruxes have been allowed to stand, so that each reader must struggle all alone with Sir Andrew's *damned colored stock* at I.iii.132, make what he can of the mysterious Lady of the Strachy at II.v.39–40, and unravel Viola's puzzling pronouncement at II.ii.12 without the aid of emendation.

In this edition the spelling has been modernized (with the exceptions noted above), the Latin act and scene divisions of the Folio translated, the punctuation brought into conformity with modern usage, a few lines that through compositorial error were printed as prose restored to verse (IV.ii.75–76), and a few stage directions (like the one at III.iv.14) shifted to accommodate the text. At the conclusion of the first, second, and fourth acts, the Folio has *"Finis Actus . . . ,"* here omitted. All editorial interpolations such as the list of characters, indications of place, and stage directions implied by the text but not indicated in the Folio are enclosed in square brackets. Other material departures from the copy text (excluding obvious typographical errors) are listed below in italic type, followed in roman by the Folio reading. It will be apparent that most of them required no agonizing reappraisal.

I.ii.15 *Arion* Orion

I.iii.29 *all most,* almost   51 *Andrew* Ma.   96 *curl by* coole my 98 *me* we   112 *kickshawses* kicke-chawses   132 *set* sit   136 *That's* That

I.iv.28 *nuncio's* Nuntio's

I.v.146 *H'as* Ha's   165 s.d. *Viola* Uiolenta   256 *with fertile tears* fertill teares   302 *County's* Countes

II.ii.20 *That sure methought* That me thought   31 *our frailty* O frailtie   32 *of* if

II.iii.26 *leman* Lemon   35 *give a—* giue a   134–35 *a nayword* an ayword

II.iv.53 *Fly . . . fly* Fye . . . fie   55 *yew* Ew   89 *I* It   104 *know—* know.

II.v.13 *metal* Mettle   115 *staniel* stallion   144 *born* become
144 *achieve* atcheeues   159–60 *thee,* THE FORTUNATE UNHAPPY./
Daylight thee, tht fortunate vnhappy daylight   177 *dear* deero

III.i.8 *king lies* Kings lyes   69 *wise men* wisemens   84 *gait* gate
93 *all ready* already   114 *here* heare

III.ii.8 *see thee the* see the   70 *renegado* Renegatho

III.iv.24 *Olivia* Mal.   73 *tang* langer   94 *How is't with you, man*
[The Folio assigns this speech to Fabian]   121 *Ay, biddy* I biddy
152 *Ay, is't,* I, ist?   181 *You . . . for't* Yon . . . fot't   256 *competent* computent

IV.ii.6 *in* in in   15 *Gorboduc* Gorbodacke   38 *clerestories* cleere
stores   73 *sport to the* sport the

V.i.201 *pavin* panyn

The Source of *Twelfth Night*

The plot of *Twelfth Night*—the adventures and misadventures of a pair of identical twins—is so old that its origins are lost in the prehistory of European literature. It had been a commonplace in Greek comedy long before Plautus and Terence imported it to Rome; and when young Shakespeare, at the start of his career, fashionably pillaged Plautus for *The Comedy of Errors,* he was following a distinguished Renaissance tradition of Italian, Spanish, French, and English writers who had worked their artful (and sometimes tedious) changes on the basic situation. One such change was the sexual differentiation of the twins, a refinement affording endless possibilities for intrigue and complication. It may be, as John Manningham suggested in the first known comment on *Twelfth Night* (see p. *xxiv* n), that for this embellishment he drew on Nicolò Secchi's *Gl'Inganni* (1562), but he could have gone to Secchi's source, which was *Gl'Ingannati* ("The Deceived"), a Plautine comedy, produced at Siena in 1531 and published six years later, that had spawned a dozen translations and adaptations through the later sixteenth century. Despite the formidable scholarship that has been brought to bear upon the question,[1] Shakespeare's knowledge of and obligation to most of this material is still a matter of dispute, but concerning his debt

[1] This scholarship is knowledgeably surveyed by Kenneth Muir, *Shakespeare's Sources,* vol. 1, *Comedies and Tragedies* (1957), pp. 66–77; and Geoffrey Bullough (ed.), *Narrative and Dramatic Sources of Shakespeare,* vol. 2 (1958), pp. 269–285.

to one late recension of *Gl'Ingannati* there is no dispute whatever. This was Barnabe Rich's "Of Apolonius and Silla," the second of a set of eight prose narratives that was published in 1581 as *Riche his Farewell to Militarie profession: conteinyng verie pleasaunt discourses fit for a peaceable tyme.*

The genealogy of "Of Apolonius and Silla" is an instructive example of the free and easy ways of sixteenth-century writers: Rich found the tale (which he eked out with incidental and unacknowledged pilferings from William Painter's *Palace of Pleasure,* a big collection of stories first published in 1566) in Pierre de Belleforest's *Histoires Tragiques* (1579), which was translated from Matteo Bandello's *Novelle* (1554), which was based on *Gl'Ingannati.* Although Shakespeare could have read, and perhaps did read, these and other cognate versions of the story, his use of the *Farewell* would seem to be established by the fact that he took from it four words—*coistrel, gaskins, pavin,* and *galliard*—that appear in *Twelfth Night* and not elsewhere in his plays. Moreover, the fifth tale in Rich's collection ("Of Two Brethren and Their Wives") supplies an analogue for the scene (IV.ii) in which Malvolio is punished, although the subplot of the arrogant steward was apparently Shakespeare's own creation. He may have drawn on other things for this or that detail— for example, on Emanuel Forde's prose romance, *The Famous History of Parismus* (1598), for the shipwreck and for the names Olivia and Violetta, or on the anonymous play *Sir Clyomon and Clamydes* (1599) for the device (which he himself had used in *The Two Gentlemen of Verona*) of a girl disguised as a man in the service of her lover—but of all the alleged or possible sources, "Of Apolonius and Silla" stands closest to *Twelfth Night,* and therefore it is here reprinted. The text, with modernized spelling and punctuation, is that of the unique copy of the 1581 edition in the Bodleian Library. The bibliographical history of the *Farewell*—a book so popular that it was reprinted in 1583, 1594, and 1606—has been treated by Thomas Mabry Cranfill in his edition of the work (1959), pp. liii–lxxxi.

Of Apolonius and Silla

THE ARGUMENT OF THE SECOND HISTORY

Apolonius Duke, having spent a year's service in the wars against the Turk, returning homeward with his company by sea, was driven by force of weather to the Isle of Cyprus, where he was well received by Pontus, governor of the same Isle; with whom Silla, daughter to Pontus, fell so strangely in love, that after Apolonius was departed to Constantinople, Silla, with one man, followed, and coming to Constantinople, she served Apolonius in the habit of a man, and after many pretty accidents falling out, she was known to Apolonius, who, in requital of her love, married her.

There is no child that is born into this wretched world but before it doth suck the mother's milk it taketh first a sup of the cup of error, which maketh us, when we come to riper years, not only to enter into actions of injury, but many times to stray from that is right and reason; but in all other things, wherein we show ourselves to be most drunken with this poisoned cup, it is in our actions of love; for the lover is so estranged from that is right, and wandereth so wide from the bounds of reason, that he is not able to deem white from black, good from bad, virtue from vice; but only led by the appetite of his own affections, and grounding them on the foolishness of his own fancies, will so settle his liking on such a one as either by desert or unworthiness will merit rather to be loathed than loved.

If a question might be asked, what is the ground indeed of reasonable love, whereby the knot is knit of true and perfect friendship, I think those that be wise would answer—desert: that is, where the party beloved doth requite us with the like; for otherwise, if the bare show of beauty or the comeliness of personage might be sufficient to confirm us in our love, those that be accustomed to go to fairs and markets might sometimes fall in love with twenty in a day. Desert must then be, of force, the ground of reasonable love; for to love them that hate us, to follow them that fly from us, to fawn on them that frown on us, to curry favor with them that disdain us, to be glad to please them that care not how they offend us, who will not confess this to be an erroneous love, neither grounded upon wit nor reason? Wherefore, right courteous gentlewomen, if it please you with patience to peruse this history following, you shall see Dame Error so play her part with a leash of lovers, a male and two females, as shall work a wonder to your wise judgment, in noting the effect of their amorous devices and conclusions of their actions—the first neglecting the love of a noble dame, young, beautiful, and fair, who only for his goodwill played the part of a serving man, contented to abide any manner of pain only to behold him. He again setting his love of a dame, that despising him (being a noble duke) gave herself to a serving man, as she had thought; but it otherwise fell out, as the substance of this tale shall better describe. And because I have been something tedious in my first discourse [i.e., "Sappho, Duke of Mantona," the first of the eight tales in Rich's *Farewell*], offending your patient ears with the hearing of a circumstance overlong, from henceforth that which I mind to write shall be done with such celerity, as the matter that I pretend to pen may in any wise permit me, and thus followeth the history.

During the time that the famous city of Constantinople remained in the hands of the Christians, amongst many other noblemen that kept their abiding in that flourishing city there was one whose name was Apolonius, a worthy duke, who being but a very young man and even then new come to his possessions, which were very great, levied a mighty band of men at his own proper charges, with whom he served against the Turk during the space of one whole year, in which time, although it were very short, this young duke so behaved himself, as well by prowess and valiance showed with his own hands, as otherwise by his wisdom and liberality used towards his soldiers, that all the world was filled with the fame of this noble duke. When he had thus spent one year's service he caused his trumpet to sound a retreat, and gathering his company together and embarking themselves, he set sail, holding his course towards Constantinople; but, being upon the sea, by the extremity of a tempest which suddenly fell, his fleet was severed, some one way, and some another; but he himself recovered the Isle of Cyprus, where he was worthily received by Pontus, duke and governor of the same isle, with whom he lodged while his ships were new repairing.

This Pontus that was lord and governor of this famous isle was an ancient duke, and had two children, a son and a daughter; his son was named Silvio, of whom hereafter we shall have further occasion to speak, but at this instant he was in the parts of Africa, serving in the wars.

The daughter her name was Silla, whose beauty was so peerless that she had the sovereignty amongst all other dames, as well for her beauty as for the nobleness of her birth. This Silla, having heard of the worthiness of Apolonius, this young duke, who besides his beauty and good graces had a certain natural allurement, that being now in his company in her father's court, she was so strangely attached with the love of Apolonius that there was nothing might content her but his presence and sweet sight; and although she saw no manner of hope to attain to that she most desired, knowing Apolonius to be but a guest, and ready to take the benefit of the next wind and to depart into a strange country, whereby she was bereaved of all possibility ever to see him again, and therefore strived with herself to leave her fondness, but all in vain; it would not be, but, like the fowl which is once limed, the more she striveth, the faster she tieth herself. So Silla was now constrained perforce her will to yield to love, wherefore from time to time she used so great familiarity with him, as her honor might well permit, and fed him with such amorous baits as the modesty of a maid could reasonably afford; which when she perceived did take but small effect, feeling herself outraged with the extremity of her passion, by the only countenance that she bestowed upon Apolonius, it might have been well perceived that the very eyes pleaded unto him for pity and remorse. But Apolonius, coming but lately from out the field from the chasing of his enemies, and his fury not yet thoroughly dissolved nor purged from his stomach, gave no regard to those amorous enticements, which, by reason of his youth, he had not been acquainted withal. But his mind ran more to hear his pilots bring news of a merry wind, to serve his turn to Constantinople, which in the end came very prosperously; and giving Duke Pontus hearty thanks for his great entertainment, taking his leave of himself and the lady Silla his daughter, departed with his company, and with a happy gale arrived at his desired port. Gentlewomen, according to my promise I will here, for brevity's sake, omit to make repetition of the long and dolorous discourse recorded by Silla for this sudden departure of her Apolonius, knowing you to be as tenderly hearted as Silla herself, whereby you may the better conjecture the fury of her fever.

But Silla, the further that she saw herself bereaved of all hope ever any more to see her beloved Apolonius, so much the more contagious were her passions, and made the greater speed to execute that she had premeditated in her mind, which was this: amongst many servants that did attend upon her, there was one whose name was Pedro, who had a long time waited upon her in her chamber, whereby she was well assured of his fidelity and trust; to that Pedro therefore she bewrayed first the fervency of her love borne to Apolonius, conjuring him in the name of the Goddess of Love herself, and binding him by the duty that a servant ought to have, that tendereth his mistress' safety and good liking, and desiring him with tears trickling down her cheeks that he would give his consent to aid

and assist her in that she had determined, which was for
that she was fully resolved to go to Constantinople, where
she might again take the view of her beloved Apolonius,
that he, according to the trust she had reposed in him,
would not refuse to give his consent, secretly to convey her
from out her father's court according as she would give
him direction, and also to make himself partaker of her
journey, and to wait upon her, till she had seen the end of
her determination.

Pedro, perceiving with what vehemency his lady and
mistress had made request unto him, albeit he saw many
perils and doubts depending in her pretense, notwithstand
ing gave his consent to be at her disposition, promising
her to further her with his best advice, and to be ready to
obey whatsoever she would please to command him. The
match being thus agreed upon, and all things prepared in
a readiness for their departure, it happened there was a
galley of Constantinople ready to depart, which Pedro
understanding, came to the captain, desiring him to have
passage for himself, and for a poor maid that was his
sister, which were bound to Constantinople upon certain
urgent affairs; to which request the captain granted, willing
him to prepare aboard with all speed, because the wind
served him presently to depart.

Pedro now coming to his mistress and telling her how
he had handled the matter with the captain, she liking
very well of the device, disguising herself into very simple
attire, stole away from out her father's court and came
with Pedro, whom now she called brother, aboard the
galley, where all things being in readiness and the wind
serving very well, they launched forth with their oars and
set sail. When they were at the sea, the captain of the
galley, taking the view of Silla, perceiving her singular
beauty he was better pleased in beholding of her face than
in taking the height either of the sun or star; and thinking
her by the homeliness of her apparel to be but some simple
maiden, calling her into his cabin, he began to break with
her after the sea fashion, desiring her to use his own cabin
for her better ease, and during the time that she remained
at the sea she should not want a bed; and then, whispering

softly in her ear, he said that for want of a bedfellow he himself would supply that room. Silla, not being acquainted with any such talk, blushed for shame but made him no answer at all. My captain, feeling such bickering within himself, the like whereof he had never endured upon the sea, was like to be taken prisoner aboard his own ship and forced to yield himself captive without any cannon shot; wherefore, to salve all sores, and thinking it the readiest way to speed, he began to break with Silla in the way of marriage, telling her how happy a voyage she had made, to fall into the liking of such a one as himself was, who was able to keep and maintain her like a gentlewoman, and for her sake would likewise take her brother into his fellowship, whom he would by some means prefer in such sort that both of them should have good cause to think themselves thrice happy, she to light of such a husband, and he to light of such a brother. But Silla, nothing pleased with these preferments, desired him to cease his talk, for that she did think herself indeed to be too unworthy such a one as he was, neither was she minded yet to marry, and therefore desired him to fix his fancy upon some that were better worthy than herself was, and that could better like of his courtesy than she could do. The captain, seeing himself thus refused, being in a great chafe, he said as followeth:

"Then, seeing you make so little account of my courtesy proffered to one that is so far unworthy of it, from henceforth I will use the office of my authority; you shall know that I am the captain of this ship and have power to command and dispose of things at my pleasure; and seeing you have so scornfully rejected me to be your loyal husband, I will now take you by force and use you at my will, and so long as it shall please me will keep you for mine own store; there shall be no man able to defend you, nor yet to persuade me from that I have determined." Silla, with these words being stroke into a great fear, did think it now too late to rue her rash attempt, determined rather to die with her own hands than to suffer herself to be abused in such sort; therefore she most humbly desired the captain so much as he could to save her credit, and seeing that she must needs be at his will and disposition, that for that present he would depart and suffer her till night, when in the dark he might take his pleasure without any manner of suspicion to the residue of his company. The captain, thinking now the goal to be more than half won, was contented so far to satisfy her request, and departed out, leaving her alone in his cabin.

Silla, being alone by herself, drew out her knife, ready to strike herself to the heart, and, falling upon her knees, desired God to receive her soul as an acceptable sacrifice for her follies, which she had so willfully committed, craving pardon for her sins; and so forth continuing a long and pitiful reconciliation to God, in the midst whereof there suddenly fell a wonderful storm, the terror whereof was such that there was no man but did think the seas would presently have swallowed them; the billows so suddenly arose with the rage of the wind that they were all glad to fall to heaving out of water, for otherwise their feeble galley had never been able to have brooked the seas. This storm continued all that day and the next night, and they being driven to put romer before the wind [i.e., to let the ship roam where it would] to keep the galley ahead the billow, were driven upon the main shore, where the galley brake all to pieces. There was every man providing to save his own life; some gat upon hatches, boards, and casks, and were driven with the waves to and fro; but the greatest number were drowned, amongst the which Pedro was one; but Silla herself being in the cabin, as you have heard, took hold of a chest that was the captain's, the which by the only providence of God brought her safe to the shore; the which when she had recovered, not knowing what was become of Pedro her man, she deemed that both he and all the rest had been drowned, for that she saw nobody upon the shore but herself; wherefore when she had a while made great lamentations, complaining her mishaps, she began in the end to comfort herself with the hope that she had to see her Apolonius, and found such means that she brake open the chest that brought her to land, wherein she found good store of coin and sundry suits of apparel that were the captain's. And now, to prevent a number of injuries that might be proffered to a woman that was left in her case, she determined to leave her own apparel and to sort herself into some of those suits, that, being taken for a man, she might pass through the country in the better safety; and as she changed her apparel, she thought it likewise convenient to change her name; wherefore, not readily happening of any other, she called herself Silvio, by the name of her own brother, whom you have heard spoken of before.

In this manner she traveled to Constantinople, where she inquired out the palace of the Duke Apolonius; and thinking herself now to be both fit and able to play the serving man, she presented herself to the Duke, craving his service. The Duke, very willing to give succor unto strangers, perceiving him to be a proper smug young man, gave him entertainment. Silla thought herself now more than satisfied for all the casualties that had happened unto her in her journey, that she might at her pleasure take but the view of the Duke Apolonius, and above the rest of his servants was very diligent and attendant upon him; the which the Duke perceiving, began likewise to grow into good liking with the diligence of his man, and therefore made him one of his chamber. Who but Silvio then was most near about him in helping of him to make him ready in a morning, in the setting of his ruffs, in the keeping of his chamber? Silvio pleased his master so well that above all the rest of his servants about him he had the greatest credit, and the Duke put him most in trust.

At this very instant there was remaining in the city a noble Dame, a widow, whose husband was but lately deceased, one of the noblest men that were in the parts of Grecia, who left his lady and wife large possessions and great livings. This lady's name was called Julina, who besides the abundance of her wealth and the greatness of her revenues had likewise the sovereignty of all the dames of Constantinople for her beauty. To this lady Julina, Apolonius became an earnest suitor; and according to the manner of wooers, besides fair words, sorrowful sighs, and piteous countenances, there must be sending of loving letters, chains, bracelets, brooches, rings, tablets, gems, jewels, and presents, I know not what. So my Duke, who in the time that he remained in the Isle of Cyprus had no skill at all in the art of love, although it were more than half proffered unto him, was now become a scholar in Love's school, and had already learned his first lesson, that is, to speak pitifully, to look ruthfully, to promise largely, to serve diligently, and to please carefully; now he was learning his second lesson, that is, to reward liberally, to give bountifully, to present willingly, and to write lovingly. Thus Apolonius was so busied in his new study that I warrant you there was no man that could challenge him for playing the truant, he followed his profession with so good a will; and who must be the messenger to carry the tokens and love letters to the lady Julina but Silvio, his man; in him the Duke reposed his only confidence, to go between him and his lady.

Now, gentlewomen, do you think there could have been a greater torment devised wherewith to afflict the heart of Silla than herself to be made the instrument to work her own mishap, and to play the attorney in a cause that made so much against herself? But Silla, altogether desirous to please her master, cared nothing at all to offend herself, followed his busines with so good a will as if it had been in her own preferment.

Julina, now having many times taken the gaze of this young youth Silvio, perceiving him to be of such excellent perfect grace, was so entangled with the often sight of this sweet temptation, that she fell into as great a liking with the man as the master was with herself; and on a time, Silvio being sent from his master with a message to the lady Julina, as he began very earnestly to solicit in his master's behalf, Julina, interrupting him in his tale, said: "Silvio, it is enough that you have said for your master; from henceforth either speak for yourself or say nothing at all." Silla, abashed to hear these words, began in her mind to accuse the blindness of love, that Julina, neglecting the good will of so noble a duke, would prefer her love unto such a one as nature itself had denied to recompense her liking.

And now, for a time leaving matters depending as you have heard, it fell out that the right Silvio indeed (whom you have heard spoken of before, the brother of Silla) was come to his father's court into the Isle of Cyprus; where, understanding that his sister was departed in manner as you have heard, conjectured that the very occasion did proceed of some liking had between Pedro her man (that was missing with her) and herself; but Silvio, who loved his sister as dearly as his own life, and the rather for that she was his natural sister, both by father and mother, so the one of them was so like the other in countenance and favor that there was no man able to discern the one from the other by their faces, saving by their apparel, the one being a man, the other a woman.

Silvio therefore vowed to his father not only to seek out his sister Silla but also to revenge the villain which he conceived in Pedro, for the carrying away of his sister; and thus departing, having traveled through many cities and towns without hearing any manner of news of those he went to seek for, at the last he arrived at Constantinople; where, as he was walking in an evening for his own recreation, on a pleasant green yard without the walls of the city, he fortuned to meet with the lady Julina, who likewise had been abroad to take the air; and as she suddenly cast her eyes upon Silvio, thinking him to be her old acquaintance, by reason they were so like one another, as you have heard before, said unto him, "Sir Silvio, if your haste be not the greater, I pray you let me have a little talk with you, seeing I have so luckily met you in this place."

Silvio, wondering to hear himself so rightly named, being but a stranger, not of above two days' continuance in the city, very courteously came towards her, desirous to hear what she would say.

Julina, commanding her train something to stand back, said as followeth: "Seeing my good will and friendly love hath been the only cause to make me so prodigal to offer that I see is so lightly rejected, it maketh me to think that men be of this condition, rather to desire those things which they cannot come by than to esteem or value of that which both largely and liberally is offered unto them; but if the liberality of my proffer hath made to seem less the value of the thing that I meant to present, it is but in your own conceit, considering how many noblemen there hath been here before, and be yet at this present, which hath both served, sued, and most humbly entreated to attain to that which to you of myself I have freely offered, and I perceive is despised, or at the least very lightly regarded."

Silvio, wondering at these words, but more amazed that she could so rightly call him by his name, could not tell what to make of her speeches, assuring himself that she was deceived and did mistake him, did think notwithstanding it had been a point of great simplicity if he should forsake that which fortune had so favorably proffered unto him, perceiving by her train that she was some lady of great honor, and viewing the perfection of her beauty and the excellency of her grace and countenance, did think it unpossible that she should be despised, and therefore answered thus:

"Madam, if before this time I have seemed to forget myself in neglecting your courtesy, which so liberally you have meant unto me, please it you to pardon what is past, and from this day forwards Silvio remaineth ready prest [i.e., eager] to make such reasonable amends as his ability may any ways permit, or as it shall please you to command."

Julina, the gladdest woman that might be to hear this joyful news, said: "Then, my Silvio, see you fail not tomorrow at night to sup with me at my own house, where I will discourse farther with you what amends you shall make me." To which request Silvio gave his glad consent, and thus they departed very well pleased. And as Julina did think the time very long till she had reaped the fruit of her desire, so Silvio, he wished for harvest before corn could grow, thinking the time as long till he saw how matters would fall out; but not knowing what lady she might be, he presently (before Julina was out of sight) demanded of one that was walking by what she was and how she was called; who satisfied Silvio in every point, and also in what part of the town her house did stand, whereby he might inquire it out.

Silvio, thus departing to his lodging, passed the night with very unquiet sleeps, and the next morning his mind ran so much of his supper that he never cared, neither for his breakfast nor dinner; and the day to his seeming passed away so slowly that he had thought the stately steeds had been tired that draw the chariot of the sun, or else some other Josua had commanded them again to stand, and wished that Phaeton had been there with a whip.

Julina, on the other side, she had thought the clock-setter had played the knave, the day came no faster forwards; but six o'clock being once stroken, recovered comfort to both parties; and Silvio, hastening himself to the palace of Julina, where by her he was friendly welcomed, and a sumptuous supper being made ready, furnished with sundry sorts of delicate dishes, they sat them down, passing the suppertime with amorous looks, loving countenances, and secret glances conveyed from the one to the other, which did better satisfy them than the feeding of their dainty dishes.

Suppertime being thus spent, Julina did think it very unfitly if she should turn Silvio to go seek his lodging in an evening, desired him therefore that he would take a bed in her house for that night; and, bringing him up into a fair chamber that was very richly furnished, she found such means that when all the rest of her household servants were abed and quiet, she came herself to bear Silvio company, where concluding upon conditions that were in question between them, they passed the night with such joy and contentation as might in that convenient time be wished for; but only that Julina, feeding too much of some one dish above the rest, received a surfeit, whereof she could not be cured in forty weeks after, a natural inclination in all women which are subject to longing and want the reason to use a moderation in their diet. But the morning approaching, Julina took her leave and conveyed herself into her own chamber; and when it was fair daylight, Silvio, making himself ready, departed likewise about his affairs in the town, debating with himself how things had happened, being well assured that Julina had mistaken him; and, therefore, for fear of further evils, determined to come no more there, but took his journey towards other places in the parts of Grecia, to see if he could learn any tidings of his sister Silla.

The Duke Apolonius, having made a long suit and never a whit the nearer of his purpose, came to Julina to crave her direct answer, either to accept of him and of such conditions as he proffered unto her, or else to give him his last farewell.

Julina, as you have heard, had taken an earnest penny of another, whom she had thought had been Silvio, the Duke's man, was at a controversy in herself, what she might do: one while she thought, seeing her occasion served so fit, to crave the Duke's good will for the marrying of his man; then again, she could not tell what displeasure the Duke would conceive, in that she should seem to prefer his man before himself, did think it best therefore to conceal the matter till she might speak with Silvio, to use his opinion how these matters should be handled; and hereupon resolving herself, desiring the Duke to pardon her speeches, said as followeth:

"Sir Duke, for that from this time forwards I am no longer of myself, having given my full power and authority over to another, whose wife I now remain by faithful vow and promise; and albeit I know the world will wonder when they shall understand the fondness of my choice, yet I trust you yourself will nothing dislike with me, sith I have meant no other thing than the satisfying of mine own contentation and liking."

The Duke, hearing these words, answered: "Madam, I must then content myself, although against my will, having the law in your own hands, to like of whom you list and to make choice where it pleaseth you."

Julina, giving the Duke great thanks, that would content himself with such patience, desired him likewise to give his free consent and good will to the party whom she had chosen to be her husband.

"Nay, surely, Madam," quoth the Duke, "I will never

give my consent that any other man shall enjoy you than myself; I have made too great account of you than so lightly to pass you away with my good will: but seeing it lieth not in me to let you, having (as you say) made your own choice, so from henceforwards I leave you to your own liking, always willing you well, and thus will take my leave."

The Duke departed towards his own house, very sorrowful that Julina had thus served him; but in the mean space that the Duke had remained in the house of Julina, some of his servants fell into talk and conference with the servants of Julina; where, debating between them of the likelihood of the marriage between the Duke and the lady, one of the servants of Julina said that he never saw his lady and mistress use so good countenance to the Duke himself as she had done to Silvio, his man, and began to report with what familiarity and courtesy she had received him, feasted him, and lodged him, and that in his opinion, Silvio was like to speed before the Duke or any other that were suitors.

This tale was quickly brought to the Duke himself, who, making better inquiry into the matter, found it to be true that was reported; and better considering of the words which Julina had used towards himself was very well assured that it could be no other than his own man that had thrust his nose so far out of joint; wherefore, without any further respect, caused him to be thrust into a dungeon, where he was kept prisoner, in a very pitiful plight.

Poor Silvio, having got intelligence by some of his fellows what was the cause that the Duke, his master, did bear such displeasure unto him, devised all the means he could, as well by mediation by his fellows, as otherwise by petitions and supplications to the Duke that he would suspend his judgment till perfect proof were had in the matter, and then if any manner of thing did fall out against him, whereby the Duke had cause to take any grief, he would confess himself worthy not only of imprisonment but also of most vile and shameful death. With these petitions he daily plied the Duke, but all in vain, for the Duke thought he had made so good proof that he was thoroughly confirmed in his opinion against his man.

But the lady Julina, wondering what made Silvio that he was so slack in his visitation, and why he absented himself so long from her presence, began to think that all was not well; but in the end, perceiving no decoction of her former surfeit, received as you have heard, and finding in herself an unwonted swelling in her belly, assuring herself to be with child, fearing to become quite bankrout of her honor, did think it more than time to seek out a father, and made such secret search and diligent inquiry that she learned the truth how Silvio was kept in prison by the Duke, his master; and minding to find a present remedy as well for the love she bare to Silvio as for the maintenance of her credit and estimation, she speedily hasted to the palace of the Duke, to whom she said as followeth:

"Sir Duke, it may be that you will think my coming to your house in this sort doth something pass the limits of modesty, the which I protest before God, proceedeth of this desire that the world should know how justly I seek means to maintain my honor; but to the end I seem not tedious with prolixity of words, not to use other than direct circumstances, know, sir, that the love I bear to my only beloved Silvio, whom I do esteem more than all the jewels in the world, whose personage I regard more than my own life, is the only cause of my attempted journey, beseeching you that all the whole displeasure, which I understand you have conceived against him, may be imputed unto my charge, and that it would please you lovingly to deal with him whom of myself I have chosen, rather for the satisfaction of mine honest liking than for the vain preeminences or honorable dignities looked after by ambitious minds."

The Duke, having heard this discourse, caused Silvio presently to be sent for and to be brought before him, to whom he said: "Had it not been sufficient for thee, when I had reposed myself in thy fidelity and the trustiness of thy service, that thou shouldst so traitorously deal with me, but since that time hast not spared still to abuse me with so many forgeries and perjured protestations, not only hateful unto me, whose simplicity thou thinkest to be such that by the plot of thy pleasant tongue thou wouldst make me believe a manifest untruth; but most abominable be thy doings in the presence and sight of God, that hast not spared to blaspheme His holy name, by calling Him to be a witness to maintain thy leasings, and so detestably wouldst thou forswear thyself in a matter that is so openly known."

Poor Silvio, whose innocence was such that he might lawfully swear, seeing Julina to be there in place, answered thus:

"Most noble Duke, well understanding your conceived grief, most humbly I beseech you patiently to hear my excuse, not minding thereby to aggravate or heap up your wrath and displeasure, protesting before God that there is nothing in the world which I regard so much or do esteem so dear as your good grace and favor; but desirous that your Grace should know my innocency, and to clear myself of such impositions wherewith I know I am wrongfully accused, which as I understand should be in the practicing of the lady Julina, who standeth here in place, whose acquittance for my better discharge now I most humbly crave, protesting before the almighty God that neither in thought, word, nor deed I have not otherwise used myself than according to the bond and duty of a servant, that is both willing and desirous to further his master's suits, which if I have otherwise said than that is true, you, Madam Julina, who can very well decide the depths of all this doubt, I most humbly beseech you to certify a truth, if I have in anything missaid or have otherwise spoken than is right and just."

Julina, having heard this discourse which Silvio had made, perceiving that he stood in great awe of the Duke's displeasure, answered thus: "Think not, my Silvio, that my coming hither is to accuse you of any misdemeanor towards your master, so I do not deny but in all such embassages wherein towards me you have been employed, you have used the office of a faithful and trusty messenger; neither am I ashamed to confess that the first day that mine eyes did behold the singular behavior, the notable courtesy, and other innumerable gifts wherewith my Silvio is endued, but that beyond all measure my heart was so inflamed, that impossible it was for me to quench the fervent love or extinguish the least part of my conceived torment before I had bewrayed the same unto him, and of my own motion craved his promised faith and loyalty of marriage; and now is the time to manifest the same unto the world, which hath been done before God and between ourselves; knowing that it is not needful to keep secret that which is neither evil done nor hurtful to any person, therefore (as I said before) Silvio is my husband by plighted faith, whom I hope to obtain without offense or displeasure of anyone, trusting that there is no man that will so far forget himself as to restrain that which God hath left at liberty for every wight, or that will seek by cruelty to force ladies to marry otherwise than according to their own liking. Fear not then, my Silvio, to keep your faith and promise which you have made unto me; and as for the rest, I doubt not things will so fall out as you shall have no manner of cause to complain."

Silvio, amazed to hear these words, for that Julina by her speech seemed to confirm that which he most of all desired to be quit of, said: "Who would have thought that a lady of so great honor and reputation would herself be the ambassador of a thing so prejudicial and uncomely for her estate! What plighted promises be these which be spoken of altogether ignorant unto me, which if it be otherwise than I have said, you sacred gods consume me straight with flashing flames of fire. But what words might I use to give credit to the truth and innocency of my cause? Ah, Madam Julina, I desire no other testimony than your own honesty and virtue, thinking that you will not so much blemish the brightness of your honor, knowing that a woman is, or should be, the image of courtesy, continency, and shamefastness, from the which so soon as she stoopeth and leaveth the office of her duty and modesty, besides the degradation of her honor, she thrust-

eth herself into the pit of perpetual infamy. And as I
cannot think you would so far forget yourself, by the
refusal of a noble duke, to dim the light of your renown
and glory, which hitherto you have maintained amongst
the best and noblest ladies, by such a one as I know
myself to be, too far unworthy your degree and calling;
so most humbly I beseech you to confess a truth, whereto
tendeth those vows and promises you speak of, which
speeches be so obscure unto me as I know not for my life
how I might understand them."

Julina, something nipped with these speeches, said:
"And what is the matter that now you make so little
account of your Julina, that being my husband indeed,
have the face to deny me, to whom thou art contracted
by so many solemn oaths? What! Art thou ashamed to
have me to thy wife? How much oughtest thou rather to
be ashamed to break thy promised faith and to have despised the holy and dreadful name of God, but that time
constraineth me to lay open that which shame rather
willeth I should dissemble and keep secret. Behold me
then here, Silvio, whom thou hast gotten with child; who,
if thou be of such honesty, as I trust for all this I shall
find, then the thing is done without prejudice or any hurt
to my conscience, considering that by the professed faith
thou didst account me for thy wife, and I received thee
for my spouse and loyal husband, swearing by the almighty God that no other than you have made the con-
quest and triumph of my chastity, whereof I crave no
other witness than yourself and mine own conscience."

I pray you, gentlewomen, was not this a foul over-
sight of Julina, that would so precisely swear so great
an oath, that she was gotten with child by one that was
altogether unfurnished with implements for such a turn.
For God's love take heed, and let this be an example to
you when you be with child, how you swear who is the
father before you have had good proof and knowledge
of the party; for men be so subtle and full of sleight that
God knoweth a woman may quickly be deceived.

But now to return to our Silvio, who, hearing an oath
sworn so divinely that he had gotten a woman with child,

was like to believe that it had been true in very deed;
but remembering his own impediment, thought it impossible that he should commit such an act, and therefore,
half in a chafe, he said, "What law is able to restrain the
foolish indiscretion of a woman that yieldeth herself to
her own desires; what shame is able to bridle or withdraw
her from her mind and madness, or with what snaffle is
it possible to hold her back from the execution of her
filthiness? But what abomination is this, that a lady of
such a house should so forget the greatness of her estate,
the alliance whereof she is descended, the nobility of her
deceased husband, and maketh no conscience to shame
and slander herself with such a one as I am, being so far
unfit and unseemly for her degree; but how horrible it is
to hear the name of God so defaced that we make no
more account, but for the maintenance of our mischiefs
we fear no whit at all to forswear His holy name, as
though He were not in all His dealings most righteous,
true, and just and will not only lay open our leasings to
the world but will likewise punish the same with sharp
and bitter scourges."

Julina, not able to endure him to proceed any further
in his sermon, was already surprised with a vehement
grief, began bitterly to cry out, uttering these speeches
following:

"Alas, is it possible that the sovereign justice of God
can abide a mischief so great and cursed? Why may I not
now suffer death rather than the infamy which I see to
wander before mine eyes? O happy and more than right
happy had I been if inconstant fortune had not devised
this treason wherein I am surprised and caught! Am I
thus become to be entangled with snares, and in the
hands of him, who, enjoying the spoils of my honor, will
openly deprive me of my fame by making me a common
fable to all posterity in time to come? Ah, traitor and discourteous wretch, is this the recompense of the honest
and firm amity which I have borne thee? Wherein have
I deserved this discourtesy? By loving thee more than
thou art able to deserve? Is it I, arrant thief, is it I upon
whom thou thinkest to work thy mischiefs? Dost thou

think me no better worth, but that thou mayest prodigally waste my honor at thy pleasure? Didst thou dare to adventure upon me, having thy conscience wounded with so deadly a treason? Ah, unhappy, and above all other most unhappy, that have so charely preserved mine honor, and now am made a prey to satisfy a young man's lust that hath coveted nothing but the spoil of my chastity and good name."

Herewithal the tears so gushed down her cheeks that she was not able to open her mouth to use any further speech.

The Duke, who stood by all this while and heard this whole discourse, was wonderfully moved with compassion towards Julina, knowing that from her infancy she had ever so honorably used herself that there was no man able to detect her of any misdemeanor otherwise than beseemed a lady of her estate; wherefore, being fully resolved that Silvio, his man, had committed this villainy against her, in a great fury drawing his rapier, he said unto Silvio:

"How canst thou, arrant thief, show thyself so cruel and careless to such as do thee honor? Hast thou so little regard of such a noble lady, as humbleth herself to such a villain as thou art, who, without any respect either of her renown or noble estate, canst be content to seek the wrack and utter ruin of her honor? But frame thyself to make such satisfaction as she requireth, although I know, unworthy wretch, that thou art not able to make her the least part of amends, or I swear by God that thou shalt not escape the death which I will minister to thee with mine own hands, and therefore advise thee well what thou doest."

Silvio, having heard this sharp sentence, fell down on his knees before the Duke, craving for mercy, desiring that he might be suffered to speak with the lady Julina apart, promising to satisfy her according to her own contentation.

"Well," quoth the Duke, "I take thy word; and therewithal I advise thee that thou perform thy promise, or otherwise I protest before God I will make thee such an example to the world that all traitors shall tremble for fear, how they do seek the dishonoring of ladies."

But now Julina had conceived so great grief against Silvio that there was much ado to persuade her to talk with him; but remembering her own case, desirous to hear what excuse he could make, in the end she agreed; and being brought into a place severally by themselves, Silvio began with a piteous voice to say as followeth:

"I know not, madam, of whom I might make complaint, whether of you or of myself, or rather of fortune, which hath conducted and brought us both into so great adversity. I see that you receive great wrong, and I am condemned against all right, you in peril to abide the bruit of spiteful tongues, and I in danger to lose the thing that I most desire; and although I could allege many reasons to prove my sayings true, yet I refer myself to the experience and bounty of your mind." And herewithal loosing his garments down to his stomach, showed Julina his breasts and pretty teats, surmounting far the whiteness of snow itself, saying: "Lo, madam, behold here the party whom you have challenged to be the father of your child; see, I am a woman, the daughter of a noble duke, who only for the love of him, whom you so lightly have shaken off, have forsaken my father, abandoned my country, and, in manner as you see, am become a serving man, satisfying myself but with the only sight of my Apolonius. And now, madam, if my passion were not vehement and my torments without comparison, I would wish that my feigned griefs might be laughed to scorn and my dissembled pains to be rewarded with flouts. But my love being pure, my travail continual, and my griefs endless, I trust, madam, you will not only excuse me of crime, but also pity my distress, the which I protest I would still have kept secret, if my fortune would so have permitted."

Julina did now think herself to be in a worse case than ever she was before, for now she knew not whom to challenge to be the father of her child; wherefore, when she had told the Duke the very certainty of the discourse which Silvio had made unto her, she departed to her own house with such grief and sorrow that she purposed never to come out of her own doors again alive, to be a wonder and mocking stock to the world.

But the Duke, more amazed to hear this strange discourse of Silvio, came unto him; whom when he had viewed with better consideration, perceived indeed that it was Silla, the daughter of Duke Pontus; and embracing her in his arms he said:

"O the branch of all virtue and the flower of courtesy itself, pardon me, I beseech you, of all such discourtesies as I have ignorantly committed towards you: desiring you that without farther memory of ancient griefs, you will accept of me, who is more joyful and better contented with your presence, than if the whole world were at my commandment. Where hath there ever been found such liberality in a lover, which, having been trained up and nourished amongst the delicacies and banquets of the court, accompanied with trains of many fair and noble ladies living in pleasure, and in the midst of delights, would so prodigally adventure yourself, neither fearing mishaps, nor misliking to take such pains, as I know you have not been accustomed unto? O liberality never heard of before! O fact that can never be sufficiently rewarded! O true love most pure and unfeigned!" Herewithal sending for the most artificial workmen, he provided for her sundry suits of sumptuous apparel, and the marriage day appointed, which was celebrated with great triumph through the whole city of Constantinople, everyone praising the nobleness of the Duke, but so many as did behold the excellent beauty of Silla gave her the praise above all the rest of the ladies in the troop.

The matter seemed so wonderful and strange that the bruit was spread throughout all the parts of Grecia, in so much that it came to the hearing of Silvio, who, as you have heard, remained in those parts to inquire of his sister; he being the gladdest man in the world, hasted to Constantinople where, coming to his sister, he was joyfully received, and most lovingly welcomed, and entertained of the Duke, his brother-in-law. After he had remained there two or three days, the Duke revealed unto Silvio the whole discourse how it happened between his sister and the

Lady Julina, and how his sister was challenged for getting a woman with child. Silvio, blushing with these words, was stricken with great remorse to make Julina amends; understanding her to be a noble lady, and was left defamed to the world through his default, he therefore bewrayed the whole circumstance to the Duke; whereof the Duke, being very joyful, immediately repaired with Silvio to the house of Julina, whom they found in her chamber, in great lamentation and mourning. To whom the Duke said, "Take courage, madam, for behold here a gentleman that will not stick both to father your child and to take you for his wife; no inferior person, but the son and heir . of a noble duke, worthy of your estate and dignity."

Julina, seeing Silvio in place, did know very well that he was the father of her child, and was so ravished with joy that she knew not whether she were awake, or in some dream. Silvio, embracing her in his arms, craving forgiveness of all that was past, concluded with her the marriage day, which was presently accomplished with great joy and contentation to all parties: and thus Silvio, having attained a noble wife, and Silla, his sister, her desired husband, they passed the residue of their days with such delight as those that have accomplished the perfection of their felicities.

Commentaries

SAMUEL JOHNSON

from *The Plays of William Shakespeare*

"Twelfth Night"

This play is in the graver part elegant and easy, and in some of the lighter scenes exquisitely humorous. Aguecheek is drawn with great propriety, but his character is, in a great measure, that of natural fatuity, and is therefore not the proper prey of a satirist. The soliloquy of Malvolio is truly comic; he is betrayed to ridicule merely by his pride. The marriage of Olivia, and the succeeding perplexity, though well enough contrived to divert on the stage, wants credibility, and fails to produce the proper instruction required in the drama, as it exhibits no just picture of life.

[On Shakespeare's Comedy]

Shakespeare engaged in dramatic poetry with the world open before him; the rules of the ancients were yet known to few; the public judgment was unformed; he had no example of such fame as might force him upon imitation, nor critics of such authority as might restrain his extravagance; he therefore indulged his natural disposition;

From *The Plays of William Shakespeare* (1765). Both selections are from Johnson's edition of Shakespeare's plays, the first from the notes on *Twelfth Night*, the second from the preface to the edition.

and his disposition, as Rymer[1] has remarked, led him to comedy. In tragedy he often writes, with great appearance of toil and study, what is written at last with little felicity; but in his comic scenes he seems to produce, without labor, what no labor can improve. In tragedy he is always struggling after some occasion to be comic; but in comedy he seems to repose, or to luxuriate, as in a mode of thinking congenial to his nature. In his tragic scenes there is always something wanting, but his comedy often surpasses expectation or desire. His comedy pleases by the thoughts and the language, and his tragedy for the greater part by incident and action. His tragedy seems to be skill, his comedy to be instinct.

The force of his comic scenes has suffered little diminution from the changes made by a century and a half, in manners or in words. As his personages act upon principles arising from genuine passion, very little modified by particular forms, their pleasures and vexations are communicable to all times and to all places; they are natural, and therefore durable. The adventitious peculiarities of personal habits are only superficial dyes, bright and pleasing for a little while, yet soon fading to a dim tinct, without any remains of former luster; but the discriminations of true passion are the colors of nature; they pervade the whole mass and can only perish with the body that exhibits them. The accidental compositions of heterogeneous modes are dissolved by the chance which combined them; but the uniform simplicity of primitive qualities neither admits increase nor suffers decay. The sand heaped by one flood is scattered by another, but the rock always continues in its place. The stream of time, which is continually washing the dissoluble fabrics of other poets, passes without injury by the adamant of Shakespeare.

---

[1] Thomas Rymer (1641–1713), a critic and scholar of strongly neo-classical bent, whose *Short View of Tragedy* (1692) contains a notorious attack on *Othello*.

WILLIAM HAZLITT

from *Characters of Shakespear's Plays*

This is justly considered as one of the most delightful of
Shakespear's comedies. It is full of sweetness and pleas-
antry. It is perhaps too good-natured for comedy. It has
little satire, and no spleen. It aims at the ludicrous rather
than the ridiculous. It makes us laugh at the follies of
mankind, not despise them, and still less bear any ill will
towards them. Shakespear's comic genius resembles the
bee, rather in its power of extracting sweets from weeds
or poisons than in leaving a sting behind it. He gives the
most amusing exaggeration of the prevailing foibles of his
characters, but in a way that they themselves, instead of
being offended at, would almost join in to humor; he
rather contrives opportunities for them to show themselves
off in the happiest lights than renders them contemptible
in the perverse construction of the wit or malice of others.
—There is a certain stage of society in which people become conscious of their peculiarities and absurdities, affect to disguise what they are, and set up pretensions to
what they are not. This gives rise to a corresponding style
of comedy, the object of which is to detect the disguises
of self-love, and to make reprisals on these preposterous
assumptions of vanity by marking the contrast between
the real and the affected character as severely as possible,
and denying to those who would impose on us for what
they are not even the merit which they have. This is the
comedy of artificial life, of wit and satire, such as we

From *Characters of Shakespear's Plays* by William Hazlitt. 2nd ed.
London: Taylor & Hessey, 1818.

see it in Congreve, Wycherley, Vanbrugh, etc. To this
succeeds a state of society from which the same sort of
affectation and pretense are banished by a greater knowledge of the world or by their successful exposure on the
stage; and which by neutralizing the materials of comic
character, both natural and artificial, leaves no comedy
at all—but *the sentimental*. Such is our modern comedy.
There is a period in the progress of manners anterior to
both these, in which the foibles and follies of individuals
are of nature's planting, not the growth of art or study;
in which they are therefore unconscious of them themselves, or care not who knows them, if they can but have
their whim out; and in which, as there is no attempt at
imposition, the spectators rather receive pleasure from
humoring the inclinations of the persons they laugh at
than wish to give them pain by exposing their absurdity.
This may be called the comedy of nature, and it is the
comedy which we generally find in Shakespear. —Whether
the analysis here given be just or not, the spirit of his
comedies is evidently quite distinct from that of the authors above mentioned, as it is in its essence the same
with that of Cervantes, and also very frequently of
Molière, though he was more systematic in his extravagance than Shakespear. Shakespear's comedy is of a pas-
toral and poetical cast. Folly is indigenous to the soil, and
shoots out with native, happy, unchecked luxuriance. Absurdity has every encouragement afforded it; and nonsense
has room to flourish in. Nothing is stunted by the churlish,
icy hand of indifference or severity. The poet runs riot in
a conceit, and idolizes a quibble. His whole object is to
turn the meanest or rudest objects to a pleasurable account. The relish which he has of a pun, or of the quaint
humor of a low character, does not interfere with the
delight with which he describes a beautiful image, or the
most refined love. The clown's forced jests do not spoil
the sweetness of the character of Viola; the same house
is big enough to hold Malvolio, the Countess, Maria, Sir
Toby, and Sir Andrew Aguecheek. For instance, nothing
can fall much lower than this last character in intellect
or morals: yet how are his weaknesses nursed and dandled

by Sir Toby into something "high fantastical," when on Sir Andrew's commendation of himself for dancing and fencing, Sir Toby answers—"Wherefore are these things hid? Wherefore have these gifts a curtain before them? Are they like to take dust like Mistress Moll's picture? Why dost thou not go to church in a galliard, and come home in a coranto? My very walk should be a jig! I would not so much as make water but in a cinque-pace. What dost thou mean? Is this a world to hide virtues in? I did think by the excellent constitution of thy leg, it was framed under the star of a galliard!" How Sir Toby, Sir Andrew, and the Clown afterwards *chirp over their cups,* how they "rouse the night owl in a catch, able to draw three souls out of one weaver!" What can be better than Sir Toby's unanswerable answer to Malvolio, "Dost thou think, because thou art virtuous, there shall be no more cakes and ale?"—In a word, the best turn is given to everything, instead of the worst. There is a constant infusion of the romantic and enthusiastic, in proportion as the characters are natural and sincere: whereas, in the more artificial style of comedy, everything gives way to ridicule and indifference, there being nothing left but affectation on one side, and incredulity on the other.—Much as we like Shakespear's comedies, we cannot agree with Dr. Johnson that they are better than his tragedies; nor do we like them half so well. If his inclination to comedy sometimes led him to trifle with the seriousness of tragedy, the poetical and impassioned passages are the best parts of his comedies. The great and secret charm of *Twelfth Night* is the character of Viola. Much as we like catches and cakes and ale, there is something that we like better. We have a friendship for Sir Toby; we patronize Sir Andrew; we have an understanding with the Clown, a sneaking kindness for Maria and her rogueries; we feel a regard for Malvolio, and sympathize with his gravity, his smiles, his cross garters, his yellow stockings, and imprisonment in the stocks. But there is something that excites in us a stronger feeling than all this—it is Viola's confession of her love.

CHARLES LAMB

[On the Character of Malvolio]

Malvolio is not essentially ludicrous. He becomes comic but by accident. He is cold, austere, repelling; but dignified, consistent, and, for what appears, rather of an overstretched morality. Maria describes him as a sort of Puritan; and he might have worn his gold chain with honor in one of our old Roundhead families, in the service of a Lambert, or a Lady Fairfax. But his morality and his manners are misplaced in Illyria. He is opposed to the proper *levities* of the piece, and falls in the unequal contest. Still his pride, or his gravity, (call it which you will) is inherent, and native to the man, not mock or affected, which latter only are the fit objects to excite laughter. His quality is at the best unlovely, but neither buffoon nor contemptible. His bearing is lofty, a little above his station, but probably not much above his deserts. We see no reason why he should not have been brave, honorable, accomplished. His careless committal of the ring to the ground (which he was commissioned to restore to Cesario) bespeaks a generosity of birth and feeling. His dialect on all occasions is that of a gentleman and a man of education. We must not confound him with the eternal old, low steward of comedy. He is master of the household to a great Princess, a dignity probably conferred upon him for other respects than age or length of service. Olivia, at the first indication of his supposed madness,

From "On Some of the Old Actors" in *Elia. Essays which have appeared under the Signature in The London Magazine* by Charles Lamb. London: Taylor & Hessey, 1823.

declares that she "would not have him miscarry for half of her dowry." Does this look as if the character was meant to appear little or insignificant? Once, indeed, she accuses him to his face—of what?—of being "sick of self-love"—but with a gentleness and considerateness which could not have been, if she had not thought that this particular infirmity shaded some virtues. His rebuke to the knight, and his sottish revelers, is sensible and spirited; and when we take into consideration the unprotected condition of his mistress, and the strict regard with which her state of real or dissembled mourning would draw the eyes of the world upon her house affairs, Malvolio might feel the honor of the family in some sort in his keeping; as it appears not that Olivia had any more brothers, or kinsmen, to look to it—for Sir Toby had dropped all such nice respects at the buttery hatch. That Malvolio was meant to be represented as possessing estimable qualities, the expression of the Duke, in his anxiety to have him reconciled, almost infers. "Pursue him, and entreat him to a peace." Even in his abused state of chains and darkness, a sort of greatness seems never to desert him. He argues highly and well with the supposed Sir Topas, and philosophizes gallantly upon his straw. There must have been some shadow of worth about the man; he must have been something more than a mere vapor—a thing of straw, or Jack in office—before Fabian and Maria could have ventured sending him upon a courting errand to Olivia. There was some consonancy (as he would say) in the undertaking, or the jest would have been too bold even for that house of misrule.

Bensley,[1] accordingly, threw over the part an air of Spanish loftiness. He looked, spake, and moved like an old Castilian. He was starch, spruce, opinionated, but his superstructure of pride seemed bottomed upon a sense of worth. There was something in it beyond the coxcomb. It was big and swelling, but you could not be sure that it was hollow. You might wish to see it taken down, but you felt that it was upon an elevation. He was magnificent from the outset; but when the decent sobrieties of the

[1] Robert Bensley (1738?–1817?), a noted actor who retired in 1796.

character began to give way, and the poison of self-love, in his conceit of the Countess's affection, gradually to work, you would have thought that the hero of La Mancha in person stood before you. How he went smiling to himself! With what ineffable carelessness would he twirl his gold chain! What a dream it was! You were infected with the illusion and did not wish that it should be removed! You had no room for laughter! If an unseasonable reflection of morality obtruded itself, it was a deep sense of the pitiable infirmity of man's nature, that can lay him open to such frenzies—but in truth you rather admired than pitied the lunacy while it lasted—you felt that an hour of such mistake was worth an age with the eyes open. Who would not wish to live but a day in the conceit of such a lady's love as Olivia? Why, the Duke would have given his principality but for a quarter of a minute, sleeping or waking, to have been so deluded. The man seemed to tread upon air, to taste manna, to walk with his head in the clouds, to mate Hyperion. O! shake not the castles of his pride—endure yet for a season, bright moments of confidence—"stand still ye watches of the element," that Malvolio may be still in fancy fair Olivia's lord—but fate and retribution say no—I hear the mischievous titter of Maria—the witty taunts of Sir Toby—the still more insupportable triumph of the foolish knight—the counterfeit Sir Topas is unmasked—and "thus the whirligig of time," as the true clown hath it, "brings in his revenges." I confess that I never saw the catastrophe of this character, while Bensley played it, without a kind of tragic interest.

HARLEY GRANVILLE-BARKER

[Director's] Preface

This play is classed, as to the period of its writing, with *Much Ado About Nothing, As You Like It,* and *Henry V.* But however close in date, in spirit I am very sure it is far from them. I confess to liking those other three as little as any plays he ever wrote. I find them so stodgily good, even a little (dare one say it?) vulgar, the work of a successful man who is caring most for success. I can imagine the lovers of his work losing hope in the Shakespeare of that year or two. He was thirty-five and the first impulse of his art had spent itself. He was popular. There was welcome enough, we may be sure, for as many *Much Ado*'s and *As You Like It*'s and jingo history pageants as he'd choose to manufacture. It was a turning point and he might have remained a popular dramatist. But from some rebirth in him that mediocre satisfaction was foregone, and, to our profit at least, came *Hamlet, Macbeth, Lear,* and the rest. *Hamlet,* perhaps, was popular, though Burbage may have claimed a just share in making it so. But I doubt if the great heart of the public would beat any more constantly towards the rarer tragedies in that century and society than it will in this. To the

From *Twelfth Night. An Acting Edition. With a Producer's Preface by Granville-Barker.* London: William Heinemann, 1912. This preface and two companion pieces written for Heinemann's acting editions of *The Winter's Tale* (1912) and *A Midsummer Night's Dream* were Granville-Barker's first attempts in the form that he later made his own. They were written in conjunction with, and no doubt reflect, his famous Savoy productions of these plays. See C. B. Purdom, *Harley Granville-Barker* (1955), pp. 150–51. Reprinted by permission of the trustees of the Granville-Barker estate.

average man or playgoer three hundred or indeed three thousand years are as a day. While we have Shakespeare's own comment even on that "supporter to a state," Polonius (true type of the official mind. And was he not indeed Lord Chamberlain?), that where art is concerned "He's for a jig, or a tale of bawdry, or he sleeps."

Twelfth Night is, to me, the last play of Shakespeare's golden age. I feel happy ease in the writing, and find much happy carelessness in the putting together. It is akin to the *Two Gentlemen of Verona* (compare Viola and Julia), it echoes a little to the same tune as the sweeter parts of the *Merchant of Venice,* and its comic spirit is the spirit of the Falstaff scenes of *Henry IV,* that are to my taste the truest comedy he wrote.

There is much to show that the play was designed for performance upon a bare platform stage without traverses or inner rooms or the like. It has the virtues of this method, swiftness and cleanness of writing and simple directness of arrangement even where the plot is least simple. It takes full advantage of the method's convenience. The scene changes constantly from anywhere suitable to anywhere else that is equally so. The time of the play's action is any time that suits the author as he goes along. Scenery is an inconvenience. I am pretty sure that Shakespeare's performance went through without a break. Certainly its conventional arrangement into five acts for the printing of the Folio is neither by Shakespeare's nor any other sensitive hand; it is shockingly bad. If one must have intervals (as the discomforts of most theaters demand), I think the play falls as easily into the three divisions I have marked as any [i.e., intervals after II.iii and IV.i].

I believe the play was written with a special cast in mind. Who was Shakespeare's clown, a sweet-voiced singer and something much more than a comic actor? He wrote Feste for him, and later the Fool in *Lear.* At least, I can conceive no dramatist risking the writing of such parts unless he knew he had a man to play them. And why a diminutive Maria—Penthesilea, the youngest wren of nine—unless it was only that the actor of the part was to be such a very small boy? I have cudgeled my brains to discover why Maria, as Maria, should be tiny, and finding no reason have ignored the point.

I believe too (this is a commonplace of criticism) that the plan of the play was altered in the writing of it. Shakespeare sets out upon a passionate love romance, perseveres in this until (one detects the moment, it is that jolly midnight revel) Malvolio, Sir Toby and Sir Andrew completely capture him. Even then, perhaps, Maria's notable revenge on the affectioned ass is still to be kept within bounds. But two scenes later he begins to elaborate the new idea. The character of Fabian is added to take Feste's share of the rough practical joke and set him free for subtler wit. Then Shakespeare lets fling and works out the humorous business to his heart's content. That done, little enough space is left him if the play is to be over at the proper hour, and, it may be (if the play was being prepared for an occasion, the famous festivity in the Middle Temple Hall or another), there was little enough time to finish writing it in either. From any cause, we certainly have a scandalously ill-arranged and ill-written last scene, the despair of any stage manager. But one can discover, I believe, amid the chaos scraps of the play he first meant to write. Olivia suffers not so much by the midway change of plan, for it is about her house that the later action of the play proceeds, and she is on her author's hands. It is on Orsino, that interesting romantic, that the blow falls.

> Why should I not, had I the heart to do it,
> Like to the Egyptian thief at point of death,
> Kill what I love?—a savage jealousy
> That sometime savors nobly.

On that fine fury of his—shamefully reduced to those few lines—I believe the last part of the play was to have hung. It is too good a theme to have been meant to be so wasted. And the revelation of Olivia's marriage to his page (as he supposes), his reconciliation with her, and the more vital discovery that his comradely love for

Viola is worth more to him after all than any high-sounding passion, is now all muddled up with the final rounding off of the comic relief. The character suffers severely. Orsino remains a finely interesting figure; he might have been a magnificent one. But there, it was Shakespeare's way to come out on the other side of his romance.

The most important aspect of the play must be viewed, to view it rightly, with Elizabethan eyes. Viola was played, and was meant to be played, by a boy. See what this involves. To that original audience the strain of make-believe in the matter ended just where for us it most begins, at Viola's entrance as a page. Shakespeare's audience saw Cesario without effort as Orsino sees him; more importantly they saw him as Olivia sees him; indeed it was over Olivia they had most to make believe. One feels at once how this affects the sympathy and balance of the love scenes of the play. One sees how dramatically right is the delicate still grace of the dialogue between Orsino and Cesario, and how possible it makes the more outspoken passion of the scenes with Olivia. Give to Olivia, as we must do now, all the value of her sex, and to the supposed Cesario none of the value of his, we are naturally quite unmoved by the business. Olivia looks a fool. And it is the common practice for actresses of Viola to seize every chance of reminding the audience that they are girls dressed up, to impress on one moreover, by childish by-play as to legs and petticoats or the absence of them, that this is the play's supreme joke. Now Shakespeare has devised one most carefully placed soliloquy where we are to be forcibly reminded that Cesario is Viola; in it he has as carefully divided the comic from the serious side of the matter. That scene played, the Viola, who does not do her best, as far as the passages with Olivia are concerned, to make us believe, as Olivia believes, that she is a man, shows, to my mind, a lack of imagination and is guilty of dramatic bad manners, knocking, for the sake of a little laughter, the whole of the play's romantic plot on the head.

Let me explain briefly the interpretation I favor of four or five other points.

I do not think that Sir Toby is meant for nothing but a bestial sot. He is a gentleman by birth, or he would not be Olivia's uncle (or cousin, if that is the relationship). He has been, it would seem, a soldier. He is a drinker, and while idleness leads him to excess, the boredom of Olivia's drawing room, where she sits solitary in her mourning, drives him to such jolly companions as he can find: Maria and Fabian and the Fool. He is a poor relation, and has been dear to Sir Andrew some two thousand strong or so (poor Sir Andrew), but as to that he might say he was but anticipating his commission as matrimonial agent. Now, dull though Olivia's house may be, it is free quarters. He is, it seems, in some danger of losing them, but if only by good luck he could see Sir Andrew installed there as master! Not perhaps all one could wish for in an uncle; but to found an interpretation of Sir Toby only upon a study of his unfortunate surname is, I think, for the actor to give us both less and more than Shakespeare meant.

I do not believe that Sir Andrew is meant for a cretinous idiot. His accomplishments may not quite stand to Sir Toby's boast of them; alas! the three or four languages, word for word without book, seem to end at *"Dieu vous garde, Monsieur."* But Sir Andrew, as he would be if he could—the scholar to no purpose, the fine fellow to no end, in short the perfect gentleman—is still the ideal of better men than he who yet can find nothing better to do. One can meet a score of Sir Andrews, in greater or less perfection, any day after a West End London lunch, doing what I believe is called "a slope down Bond."

Fabian, I think, is not a young man, for he hardly treats Sir Toby as his senior; he is the cautious one of the practical jokers, and he has the courage to speak out to Olivia at the end. He treats Sir Andrew with a certain respect. He is a family retainer of some sort; from his talk he has to do with horses and dogs.

Feste, I feel, is not a young man either. There runs through all he says and does that vein of irony by which we may so often mark one of life's self-acknowledged failures. We gather that in those days, for a man of parts without character and with more wit than sense, there was a kindly refuge from the world's struggle as an allowed fool. Nowadays we no longer put them in livery.

I believe Antonio to be an exact picture of an Elizabethan seaman-adventurer, and Orsino's view of him to be just such as a Spanish grandee would have taken of Drake. "Notable pirate and salt-water thief," he calls him.

> A bawbling vessel was he captain of,
> For shallow draught and bulk unprizable;
> With which such scathful grapple did he make
> With the most noble bottom of the fleet,
> That very envy and the tongue of loss
> Cried fame and honor of him.

And Antonio is a passionate fellow as those West Countrymen were. I am always reminded of him by the story of Richard Grenville chewing a wineglass in his rage.

The keynotes of the poetry of the play are that it is passionate and it is exquisite. It is life, I believe, as Shakespeare glimpsed it with the eye of his genius in that half-Italianized court of Elizabeth. Orsino, Olivia, Antonio, Sebastian, Viola are passionate all, and conscious of the worth of their passion in terms of beauty. To have one's full laugh at the play's comedy is no longer possible, even for an audience of Elizabethan experts. Though the humor that is set in character is humor still, so much of the salt of it, its play upon the time and place, can have no savor for us. Instead we have learned editors disputing over the existence and meaning of jokes at which the simplest soul was meant to laugh unthinkingly. I would cut out nothing else, but I think I am justified in cutting those pathetic survivals.

Finally, as to the speaking of the verse and prose. The prose is mostly simple and straightforward. True, he could no more resist a fine-sounding word than, as has been said, he could resist a pun. They abound, but if we have any taste for the flavor of a language he makes us delight in them equally. There is none of that difficult involuted decoration for its own sake in which he reveled in the later plays. The verse is still regular, still lyrical in its inspiration, and it should I think be spoken swiftly. . . .

I think that all Elizabethan dramatic verse must be spoken swiftly, and nothing can make me think otherwise. My fellow workers acting in *The Winter's Tale* were accused by some people (only by some) of gabbling. I readily take that accusation on myself, and I deny it. Gabbling implies hasty speech, but our ideal was speed, nor was the speed universal, nor, but in a dozen well-defined passages, really so great. Unexpected it was, I don't doubt; and once exceed the legal limit, as well accuse you of seventy miles an hour as twenty-one. But I call in question the evidence of mere policemen-critics. I question a little their expertness of hearing, a little too their quickness of understanding Elizabethan English not at its easiest, just a little their lack of delight in anything that is not as they thought it always would be, and I suggest that it is more difficult than they think to look and listen and remember and appraise all in the same flash of time. But be all the shortcomings on one side and that side ours, it is still no proof that the thing come short of is not the right thing. That is the important point to determine, and for much criticism that has been helpful in amending what we did and making clearer what we should strive towards —I tender thanks.

The Winter's Tale, as I see its writing, is complex, vivid, abundant in the variety of its mood and pace and color, now disordered, now at rest, the product of a mind rapid, changing, and overfull. I believe its interpretation should express all that. *Twelfth Night* is quite other. Daily, as we rehearse together, I learn more what it is and should be; the working together of the theater is a fine thing. But, as a man is asked to name his stroke at billiards, I will even now commit myself to this: its serious mood is passionate, its verse is lyrical, the speaking of it needs swiftness and fine tone; not rush, but rhythm, constant and compelling. And now I wait contentedly to be told that less rhythmic speaking of Shakespeare has never been heard.

October 27, 1912.

JOHN DOVER WILSON

"Twelfth Night"

The earliest recorded performance of *Twelfth Night* took place in one of the London colleges of law called the Middle Temple, on February 1602—360 years ago. The association with the Inns of Court is significant, since there are a number of little points in the play which suggest such an audience—an audience of law students. But, if so, it was probably originally written for one of the other Inns, inasmuch as it clearly followed close upon *As You Like It,* and there are literary and historical clues which point to 1600. Some have supposed that it was first produced in the late autumn of 1599, under the title of *What You Will,* which corresponds with *As You Like It* and *Much Ado about Nothing;* and that it was then given again at court before the Queen on Twelfth Night, 1600.

As there is nothing about Twelfth Night in the play, the title seems to have been derived from the fact that it was performed on that day—the greatest feast day in the year in London, the culmination of the Christmas festivities. We may suppose that it had to be renamed because it would have been hardly polite to present a play at Court with an offhand label like "What You Will." Yet, though the actual feast is not mentioned in the text, the play is preeminently one for a feast of some kind. It

From *Shakespeare's Happy Comedies* by John Dover Wilson. Evanston, Ill.: Northwestern University Press; London: Faber & Faber, Ltd., 1962. Copyright © 1962 by John Dover Wilson. Reprinted by permission of the publishers.

is full of merriment and high jinks, to say nothing of the drinking scenes, while the spirit of the whole is embodied in the Fool, whose name Feste is the contemporary French for *"fête."*

The text, too, though unusually straightforward for a Shakespearian play, shows some signs of slight revision, as if it had had to be adapted for different occasions. The most striking of these is one which suggests that originally the songs in the play were sung, not by Feste as now, but by Viola. She tells the Captain in the second scene:

> I'll serve this duke [i.e., Orsino].
> Thou shalt present me as an eunuch to him.
> It may be worth thy pains; for I can sing
> And speak to him in many sorts of music.

While at the opening of II.iv, we actually find Orsino bidding Cesario (i.e., Viola) to sing

> That old and antic song we heard last night—

though the song is sung by Feste immediately after, and though Feste does not belong to Orsino's household at all, but to Olivia's. At first sight it looks as if the voice of the boy who took Viola had become "cracked i' th' ring" since the play was originally put on, and that Armin who took Feste had to step into the breach. But Armin, who as Sir Andrew declares, "has an excellent breast," sings "O, mistress mine" in II.iii, which can never at any stage of the play's evolution have fallen to Viola's part, and that suggests revision to take advantage of his singing powers, the quality of which had not seemingly been realized when he played Touchstone, since the only singing the Fool is given in *As You Like It* is his part with the two boys in "It was a lover and his lass."[1]

---

[1] See C. J. Sisson, *New Readings in Shakespeare* (1956), vol. i, pp. 188–91, for a topical interpretation of "The Lady of the Strachy," etc. (II.v.39f.) which, if it became accepted, would imply a revision, or at least an interpolation, later than 1616, the year of Shakespeare's death. An astonishing reflection on the text of the First Folio, to say the least of it.

Apart from all this, *Twelfth Night* like *As You Like It* casts back to Shakespeare's early plays and has points of affinity both with *The Comedy of Errors* and with *The Two Gentlemen of Verona*. We find ourselves in Illyria, once again by the shores of the Mediterranean, the sea of Plautus and Terence, of Ariosto and Grazzini,[2] and though there are no actual merchants in the play, we have a couple of sea captains, one of them a "notable pirate," while (as in *Errors*) a wreck separates twin children, this time boy and girl, whose presence in the play, unknown to each other, leads to much confusion. Even details, e.g., that one of the twins is tied to a mast, are the same, while Sebastian, like Antipholus of Syracuse, sees the sights of the town upon arrival and names as his rendezvous an inn, in *Errors* "the Centaur where we host," in *Twelfth Night* "the Elephant" (is this the modern Elephant and Castle?) "in the south suburbs."

On the other hand, *Twelfth Night* has much in common with *The Two Gentlemen*. In both a forlorn lady, disguised as a page, serves the man she loves in the courtship of another woman; and in both the lady finds her rival falling in love with herself. Here, however, Shakespeare is doing more than merely repeating himself; he is again drawing upon a common source for both plays, viz. the story of Felix and Felismena, told in Jorge de Montemayor's *Diana*. Furthermore, the love-sick Orsino belongs wholly to the romantic tradition, while the devotion of Antonio, the sea captain, for Sebastian recalls that of Valentine for Proteus in *The Two Gentlemen* and of Antonio, the merchant of Venice, for his Bassanio. Again, while Olivia is a very different character from Portia, her household has some correspondence with that at Belmont. So much for the texture of the canvas upon which Shakespeare painted. What matters to us now is the completed picture.

Notice first of all then to what rich and delicate ends he here turns the device of disguise originally used in *The Two Gentlemen* but repeated with variations in every comedy since then. Like the heroine of *As You Like It*

2 See Bond, *Early Plays from the Italian* (1911), pp. xix–xxvi.

the heroine of *Twelfth Night* is dressed as a girl in the
second scene, but becomes a boy for the rest of the play.
Yet Viola makes a very different boy from Rosalind;
there is nothing of the "saucey lackey" about her; she
never even assumes the swagger of the man except in
the scuffle with Maria in the first interview with Olivia.
On the contrary, the whole charm of the part is the gentle
girlhood that breathes behind the male doublet. And if
there be any who, with Meredith, tend to despise Shakespeare's "incredible imbroglio," let them imagine *Twelfth
Night* without disguise and ask how Shakespeare could
have got his effects in any other way. The scenes between
Viola and Orsino (II.iv.80–124) and between Viola and
Olivia (I.v.220–89; III.i.94–166) depend entirely upon
the disguise, and they are the subtlest and loveliest scenes
in the play. Their emotional quality, as of fine-spun silk,
is shot with crosslights and shifting color. The Duke,
sick with hopeless passion for Olivia, discussing Love
with the disguised Viola, sick with passion for him,[3] com-
pose a situation in which tenderness, beauty and "the
slim feasting smile" of the comic muse are perfectly
blended.

One passage to remind the reader of it. The Duke
sends Cesario a second time to urge his suit with Olivia:

VIOLA. But if she cannot love you, sir?

DUKE. I cannot be so answered.

VIOLA.   Sooth, but you must.
  Say that some lady, as perhaps there is,
  Hath for your love as great a pang of heart
  As you have for Olivia: you cannot love her;
  You tell her so; must she not then be answered?

DUKE. There is no woman's sides
  Can bide the beating of so strong a passion
  As love doth give my heart; no woman's heart
  So big, to hold so much; they lack retention.

[3] In the passionate service of Pyrocles by Zelmane disguised as a page
Sidney gave Shakespeare a hint for this in *Arcadia* (1590), Lib. 2, pp.
290 ff.

Alas, their love may be called appetite—
No motion of the liver, but the palate—
That suffers surfeit, cloyment and revolt;
But mine is all as hungry as the sea,
And can digest as much. Make no compare
Between that love a woman can bear me
And that I owe Olivia.

VIOLA.   Ay, but I know—

DUKE. What dost thou know?

VIOLA. Too well what love women to men may owe:
In faith they are as true of heart as we.
My father had a daughter loved a man,
As it might be, perhaps, were I a woman,
I should your lordship.

DUKE.   And what's her history?

VIOLA. A blank, my lord: she never told her love,
But let concealment like a worm i' th' bud
Feed on her damask cheek; she pined in thought,
And with a green and yellow melancholy
She sat like Patience on a monument,
Smiling at grief. Was not this love, indeed?
We men may say more, swear more—but indeed
Our shows are more than will; for still we prove
Much in our vows, but little in our love.

DUKE. But died thy sister of her love, my boy?

VIOLA. I am all the daughters of my father's house,
And all the brothers too ... and yet I know not ...
Sir, shall I to this lady?

DUKE. (*starts and rouses*). Ay, that's the theme.
To her in haste; give her this jewel; say,
My love can give no place, bide no delay. (*They go*.[4]

Scarcely less poignantly humorous are the scenes in
which Olivia, courted for Orsino by Viola, falls in love
with the messenger. And both situations have the same

4 II.iv.88–125.

root—the contrast between Love and Fancy—Love,
genuine, tender and appealing, embodied in the wistful
figure of the slender Cesario—and Fancy in the persons
of Orsino, the melancholy egoist, and Olivia, the willful
recluse.

> Tell me where is Fancy bred,
> Or in the heart or in the head?
> How begot, how nourishèd?
> > Reply, reply.
> It is engend'red in the eyes,
> With gazing fed; and Fancy dies
> In the cradle where it lies.
> > Let us all ring Fancy's knell:
> > I'll begin it,—Ding, dong, bell.

Such we found was Shakespeare's comment upon Sentimentalism (a word not then invented) in *The Merchant
of Venice*. In *Twelfth Night* he devotes a whole play to
the subject.

Orsino is the sentimentalist in love with Love. He has
steeped himself, we may imagine, in Petrarch; he prefers
worshiping at a distance, and wooing by proxy; he likes
to stab himself with the thought of the cruelty of his
adored. It is not Olivia's person he desires—he readily
makes shift with Viola at the end, when Olivia proves to
be the bride of another. It is the dream of her that fills
him with melancholy satisfaction. Viola will make him
a good wife, because she wants *him* and is the soul of
loyalty and devotion. But will he make her a good husband? It is significant that in his last words he hails her as

> Orsino's mistress and his *fancy's* queen.

She is Laura still, as Olivia had been. But can one marry
Laura and retain the Fancy? Your sentimentalist is sel-
dom contented with

> A creature not too bright and good
> For human nature's daily food.

The opening scene of the play gives us, indeed, all we need to know about Orsino.

> If music be the food of love, play on,
> Give me excess of it; that, surfeiting,
> The appetite may sicken and so die . . .
> That strain again! it had a dying fall;
> O, it came o'er my ear like the sweet south[5]
> That breathes upon a bank of violets;
> Stealing and giving odor. [*music*] Enough, no more!
> 'Tis not so sweet now as it was before.
> O spirit of love, how quick and fresh art thou,
> That, notwithstanding thy capacity
> Receiveth as the sea, nought enters there,
> Of what validity and pitch soe'er,
> But falls into abatement and low price,
> Even in a minute . . . So full of shapes is fancy,
> That it alone is high fantastical.

Lovely lines—one of the loveliest openings in all Shakespeare's plays. Yet the loveliness must not be allowed to hide the meaning from us, which has been almost universally misunderstood. Orsino is generally supposed to be wishing that his love may die of a surfeit and so cease to trouble him. But this, as a matter of fact, is the last thing he would desire. He is acclaiming the tyranny of love, which accepts all offerings but at the same time makes them seem worthless. He does not value music for itself but as the temporary food for his love, which is "all as hungry as the sea, And can digest as much."[6] He has to keep feeding Love, as best he can; and when Love's appetite for this or that dies, he must turn to something else, as indeed he does in the last words of the scene, which concludes:

> Away before me to sweet beds of flowers—
> Love-thoughts lie rich when canopied with bowers.

[5] Pope's emendation of F "sound"; Steevens cites *Arcadia* (1590), Lib. i, p. 7. "Her breath is more sweet than a gentle south-west wind which comes creeping over flowrie fieldes . . . in the extreeme heate of summer." This renders Pope's "south" almost certain.
[6] II.iv.101–02.

His constancy is but the excuse for a variety of emotional self-indulgence. For, as Feste exclaims upon him, "Now, the melancholy god protect thee, and the tailor make thy doublet of changeable taffeta, for thy mind is a very opal."[7] He is the epicurean lover, ever seeking, not the satisfaction of his desires, but their perpetuation. Olivia, Viola, womankind in general, are a means not an end. They exist, not as objects to be attained but as stimulants, stimulants which induce that intoxicating mood of yearning, melancholy, and despair in which his spirit delights.

Orsino's is the lover's melancholy; Jaques despises love, and has a melancholy of his own "compounded of many simples." Yet they are variant specimens of the same breed; and their affinity comes out best in their attitude towards music. For Orsino like Jaques can "suck melancholy out of a song as a weasel sucks eggs."

Orsino and Jaques are two studies in sentimentalism. And Olivia is another. True, she has lost father and brother, both deeply beloved, within a twelvemonth. But she cannot "let the dead bury their dead," and decides, like Victoria, the Widow of Windsor, to feed upon her sorrow. We are told:

> The element itself, till seven years hence,
> Shall not behold her face at ample view;
> But like a cloistress she will veilèd walk,
> And water once a day her chamber round
> With eye-offending brine; all this to season
> A brother's dead love, which she would keep fresh
> And lasting, in her sad remembrance.[8]

It is an attitude which Orsino, of course, much admires, even while he complains of her cruelty towards himself. It takes the Fool to tell her the rude truth:

> CLOWN. Good madonna, give me leave to prove you a
> fool.
>
> OLIVIA. Can you do it?

7 II.iv.73 ff.
8 I.i.27–33.

CLOWN. Dexteriously, good madonna.

OLIVIA. Make your proof.

CLOWN. I must catechize you for it, madonna. Good my
mouse of virtue, answer me.

OLIVIA. Well, sir, for want of other idleness, I'll bide your
proof.

CLOWN. Good madonna, why mourn'st thou?

OLIVIA. Good fool, for my brother's death.

CLOWN. I think his soul is in hell, madonna.

OLIVIA. I know his soul is in heaven, fool.

CLOWN. The more fool, madonna, to mourn for your
brother's soul, being in heaven . . . Take away the
fool, gentlemen![9]

Olivia is a gentler Constance, to whom King Philip
shrewdly remarks, after one of her outbursts of sorrow for
Prince Arthur,

>   You are as fond of grief as of your child.

Olivia is as fond of grief as of her brother, and in her
extravagant vow of seven years' seclusion, and her abjur-
ing "the company and sight of men," she reminds us of
the students in *Love's Labor's Lost,* who vow to observe
a three years' seclusion in their little academe from the
society of women. Such vows, with which men bind themselves in their self-conceit and in defiance of nature, cannot last, and hers endures no longer than theirs. No
sooner does a young man (as she takes Viola to be) appear before her than she falls head over ears in love, and
it is with delicate irony that Shakespeare makes her plight
her troth with Viola's twin in the very chantry that she had
erected to her brother's memory—a point, I think, usually
overlooked by readers and spectators. Another subtle
point, often likewise overlooked, is that, as Malvolio
informs us, Olivia's seal is an intaglio of Lucrece, the

9 I.v.56–71.

classical type of chastity. Clearly, she had elaborated her dedicated life into a system.

These two sentimentalists, the opal-minded lover of Love and the cypress-clad lover of Sorrow, make, as it were, the poles of the Illyrian world. They sit apart, he in his palace, she in hers, each in an isolation exquisitely ridiculous—and Viola passes from one to the other. Viola acts as foil to both, and as touchstone to their unrealities. For Viola, like Rosalind, carries fresh air with her wherever she goes; she is compact of sweetness and common sense; and when she loves, she loves flesh and blood. Thus true Love, hiding herself behind her disguise, and eating her heart out in simple humility of spirit, links the houses of the two Fancy-mongers. It is a pretty pattern.

But there's more in it even than that. There is Malvolio, the chief character in the underplot, or anti-masque; the comic underplot which reflects in a kind of distorting mirror the emotional situation of the main plot. For Malvolio is a dreamer, after his kind; like Orsino he aspires for the hand of Olivia; and like both Orsino and Olivia he mistakes dreams for realities. When Maria tells Sir Toby that "he has been yonder i' the sun practicing behavior to his own shadow,"[10] she goes near to the heart of this shadow-dance of a play—Orsino, Olivia and Malvolio all, in different fashion, practice behavior to their own shadows. And when Olivia[11] tells Malvolio that he is "sick of self-love," she puts her finger on one of the roots of her own sickness and of Orsino's. They are all three egoists, though they wear their egoism with a difference.

The Elizabethans would have called them three melancholics. The melancholy of Malvolio is a fantastic ambition. He is not, of course, in love with Olivia. He dreams of becoming her husband as a means of becoming the lord of her house; and his distempered imagination is constantly presenting him with visions of himself in that exalted position. "Having been three months married to her," he muses in the garden,

10 II.v.15–16.
11 I.v.90.

sitting in my state, calling my officers about me, in my
branched velvet gown; having come from a daybed,
where I have left Olivia sleeping. And then to have the
humor of state: and after a demure travel of regard,
telling them I know my place, as I would they should do
theirs, to ask for my kinsman Toby. Seven of my people,
with an obedient start, make out for him: I frown the
while, and perchance wind up my watch, or play with
my [*touches his steward's chain an instant, and then
starts*] some rich jewel.[12]

Differences of rank meant so much to the men of that
time—so incalculably much more than they do to us—
that the dreams of Malvolio would have seemed to them
preposterous to a degree which we are unable to ap-
preciate. And in a play by anyone but Shakespeare he
would appear to a twentieth-century audience a rather
stupid butt, upon which an amusing practical joke is
played by Maria, and that is all. But in Shakespeare's
hands his dream blossoms into a monstrous beauty, ex-
pressed in all the magnificent magniloquence of post-
Falstaffian prose, a beauty which rivals in its fashion that
of Shylock's rhetoric or even Falstaff's itself. As with Shylock, so with Malvolio: Shakespeare let himself go, to the
risk of wrenching the drama out of frame.

Malvolio is the most interesting—I was going to say,
the largest-souled—character in the play. Lytton Strachey's
earliest, and I think his best, book—the masterly little
Landmarks in French Literature—contains a comparison
between the characters of Malvolio and Tartuffe which is
worth quoting in this connection:

The narrowed and selective nature of Molière's treatment
of character presents an illuminating contrast when compared with the elaborately detailed method of such a
master of the romantic style as Shakespeare. The English
dramatist shows his persons to us in the round; innumerable facets flash out quality after quality; the subtlest
and most elusive shades of temperament are indicated;

12 II.v.44–61. The stage direction, surely right, was suggested by Brinsley
Nicholson.

until at last the whole being takes shape before us, endowed with what seems to be the very complexity and mystery of life itself. Entirely different is the great Frenchman's way. Instead of expanding, he deliberately narrows his view; he seizes upon two or three salient qualities in a character and then uses all his art to impress them indelibly upon our minds. His Harpagon is a miser, and he is old—and that is all we know about him: how singularly limited a presentment, compared with that of Shakespeare's bitter, proud, avaricious, and almost pathetic Jew! Tartuffe, perhaps the greatest of all Molière's characters, presents a less complex figure even than such a slight sketch as Shakespeare's Malvolio. Who would have foreseen Malvolio's exquisitely preposterous address to Jove? In Tartuffe there are no such surprises; he displays three qualities, and three only—religious hypocrisy, lasciviousness, and the love of power; and there is not a word he utters which is not impregnated with one or all of these. . . .

His [Molière's] method is narrow, but it is deep. He rushes to the essentials of a human being—tears out his vitals, as it were—and, with a few repeated masterstrokes, transfixes the naked soul. . . . Nor is it only by its vividness that his portraiture excels. At its best it rises into the region of sublimity, giving us new visions of the grandeur to which the human spirit can attain.[13]

I have quoted this much, not only because I think Strachey's distinction between the methods of Shakespeare and Molière both useful and penetrating, but also because I consider that, different as their methods are, Shakespeare and Molière achieve similar results in their creation of Malvolio and Tartuffe. Both characters, however we may laugh at the one's absurdity and detest the other's vices, raise us "into the region of sublimity." And just because this is so, some readers and spectators find the treatment meted out to Malvolio and the dark-house scenes intolerable.

There is no evidence that Shakespeare himself felt any

13 Lytton Strachey, *Landmarks in French Literature* (Home University Library). pp. 82–4.

tenderness for Malvolio, as he obviously did for some of his other fantastics, e.g., for Mistress Quickly or Master Slender, for Armado or even the odious Parolles. The character is drawn as coldly and as objectively as that of Holofernes, or as that of Jaques, with which as a matter of fact Malvolio has some affinity.

The letter scene in the garden is a thing of sheer delight, and Malvolio's behavior is so "exquisitely preposterous" that our laughter goes wholly against him. But when we come to the mad scene, we begin to feel that the jest has been "refined even to pain," and our sympathies veer towards the victim, despite the excellent fooling of Feste with his two voices. Here we must recollect that madness has longed ceased to be comic to us, as it was to the Elizabethans, who flocked to Bedlam for amusement as Londoners now flock to the monkey-house at the Zoo. But this does not excuse Shakespeare, if excuse be needed.

It is more to the point to stress the significance of Malvolio's appearance in the final scene. There he is allowed to say his say in his own defense in a letter to his mistress and an indignant speech, both couched in language of great dignity, without a touch of cringing or a false note of any kind, so that we feel that, awaked from his dream, he is after all a man of spirit and self-respect. But his thirst for revenge somewhat alienates us again.

Moreover Olivia knows him well, and values him as an admirable steward; had, indeed, declared when she thinks he is really mad, "I would not have him miscarry for the half of my dowry." Once the whole plot against him has been exposed, she pities him and implicitly condemns the jest as a sorry one. "Alas, poor fool! how have they baffled thee" bursts from her lips at the end of Fabian's explanation, while after Malvolio's exit she declares, "He hath been most notoriously abused." These words, coming as they do at the very end of the play, prove I think that Shakespeare intended us to realize that Malvolio had a case, and that while he has himself no affection for him, he acknowledges that less than justice had been meted out to him.

To speak dramatically, having made excellent use of

him as the butt of his comic scene in the garden, he later deliberately adjusted the balance of our sympathies in his favor.[14] There are some to whom a dramatic issue left indecisive is anathema; they think Shakespeare must take sides, must exhibit his sympathy with this character or that, with this attitude or that. If so—surely, the less dramatist he! As we saw in Chapter V, Shakespeare takes sides neither for nor against Shylock, he shows us the issue, forces us indeed to contemplate it in all its hideous reality and its apparently hopeless irreconcilability, and leaves it at that. So, in a less intense degree, with Malvolio. For the Malvolio-Sir Toby antithesis stands for a great human issue scarcely less significant than that which concerns Shylock and Antonio. "Marry, sir," declares Maria to Sir Toby, "sometimes he is a kind of puritan." And though she goes on to say, "The devil a puritan that he is, or anything constantly but a time-pleaser, an affectioned ass,"[15] Shakespeare has dropped his hint, which is supported by Fabian's hint later that Malvolio is an opponent of bearbaiting (a sport against which the puritans, all honor to them for it, waged a constant war).[16] Malvolio is not a typical puritan—that was Ben Jonson's way, not Shakespeare's. But he is somewhat of that way of thinking, and he quite obviously stands for order and sobriety in the commonwealth of Olivia's household.

Further, he has the defects of his qualities, the defects that so often afflict the puritan, the revolutionary, the social reformer: viz., absence of humor, intolerance of the innocent pleasures of life, and belief that order, seemliness, and respectability are the greatest things, if not the only things, that matter; and, together with all this, a firm conviction that he, Malvolio, is the true representative of order, the heaven-directed censor and corrector of the morals and habits of other people. Not all this, perhaps, is explicit in the text; but it is all, I think, implied. Certainly,

14 It is of course a great part for an actor, and Professor Alexander reminds us that Charles Lamb "could never see Bensley play that character without feeling in it a tragic dignity." (See *Elia*, 1823, "On Some of the Old Actors," and Alexander, *Shakespeare's Life and Art*, pp. 64–5.)

15 II.iii.140, 146–47.

16 Cf. Slender's attitude in *The Merry Wives*, I.i.273–4.

the famous and unexpected cry of "Jove, I thank thee!" after the perusal of the supposed letter from Olivia, suggests just that intimacy with the Almighty which persons of his serene self-assurance are wont to assume.

On the other hand, while Sir Toby is hardly the typical cavalier, he too, quite obviously, shares the cavalier attitude towards life, or, shall we say, the somewhat disreputable side of it, a closer kinsman indeed of Falstaff's than the Sir John of that family in *The Merry Wives of Windsor*. He is "sure care's an enemy to life"; he hates "a false conclusion . . . as an unfilled can":[17] with him it is always too late to go to bed at night, and never too early to get drunk in the morning. Yet he has the ruins of gentry about him, together with the dregs of learning. He speaks Spanish (or is it Italian?) on one occasion,[18] French on another, and Latin on a third;[19] he knows more about contemporary physiology than most modern editors; he talks theology in his cups; and is prepared to discuss "philosophy," i.e., science, when there is no drink at hand to discuss.[20] And his boon companions, the foolish Sir Andrew Aguecheek, and the wiser Feste, together with Fabian—all enemies of Malvolio—are of the party of Misrule also. The "thin-faced"[21] Sir Andrew, is cousin-german to Slender of *The Merry Wives* and was doubtless played by the same actor; but he has little of Slender's attractiveness. Fabian calls him Sir Toby's "manakin" (III.ii.54), and the name fits excellently, since the knight manipulates him like a puppet. He evidently too delights in his sheer fatuity, though he delights still more in the "three thousand ducats a year" (I.iii.22) which he does his best to help him spend. Dramatically, Sir Andrew and Sir Toby are linked together like Siamese twins.

Very different is Feste, the subtlest of all Shakespeare's Fools, about whom I shall have more to say in a minute.

17 I.iii.2–3; II.iii.6.
18 I.iii.42–43, *"Castiliano vulgo"* for which Henry Thomas conjectured (*Times Literary Supplement*, 4/6/33), *"Castiglione voglio"* = "I want some Castiglione," a costly wine, alternatively known as Lacrima Christi.
19 II.iii.2.
20 See note on II.iii.11 in my edition.
21 V.i.207.

Here I would only note that the scenes involving the Fool and Sir Toby to some extent reflect the old medieval custom of appointing a Lord of Misrule, who was responsible for the revels between Christmas and Twelfth Night at court and other places. Sir Toby is clearly the Lord of Misrule in Olivia's household, and Feste, as I have said above, stands as it were for the very spirit of Christmas revelry. Now the great enemy of all these old customs and festivals, which they were doing their best to suppress throughout the land, were of course the puritans. It is therefore no accident that Shakespeare gives to Sir Toby and Feste the immortal, unanswerable, retort to Malvolio and his kind:

SIR TOBY. Dost thou think because thou art virtuous, there shall be no more cakes and ale?

FESTE. Yes, by Saint Anne, and ginger shall be hot i' th' mouth too.[22]

In the clash between the precise steward and the caterwauling kinsman, you have the puritan-cavalier issue in little, the issue which was beginning to divide England during Shakespeare's lifetime, which led to civil war shortly after his death, and which is even yet undecided. I am not claiming that Shakespeare is also among the prophets, still less that he deliberately set out to illustrate a thesis in his Toby-Malvolio scenes; only that, having a riotous knight and an orderly-minded steward upon his hands, the dramatic conflict between them quite naturally took a form which illustrated the prevailing tendencies of the time. In other words the supersensitive imagination of a supreme dramatic artist so penetrates to the root of an issue presented to him by his plot that his exposition of it, without his being perhaps in the least conscious of the fact, becomes a comment upon the main problem of his age.

Such things are not unparalleled in modern literature. In the novels of Dostoevsky, for example, you may catch glimpses of the spiritual development of Russia and of Europe for half a century after they were written. In

[22] II.iii.114-17.

particular, *The Possessed* foreshadows in unmistakable terms the Bolshevik revolution which did not take place for another fifty years.

But it is a little ridiculous to speak of Dostoevsky in relation to *Twelfth Night*. We must not take Malvolio too seriously; for assuredly Shakespeare did not. He is only part of the dramatic composition, the total effect of which is one of gaiety and high festival.

How much, for example, does music mean in this play? More, curiously, than in *As You Like It,* which has twice as many songs. It begins

> If music be the food of love, play on,

and ends with

> When that I was and a little tiny boy,
>   With hey, ho, the wind and the rain;
> A foolish thing was but a toy,
>   For the rain it raineth every day,

while between them lie two of Shakespeare's loveliest songs:

> O, mistress mine, where are you roaming?
>   (II.iii.40ff.)

and

> Come away, come away death.   (II.iv.51ff.)

The music as constantly accompanies Orsino, as the kettledrums do Claudius in *Hamlet*. And there is all the music of Shakespeare's verse, at its ripest and sweetest, at the turn of the tide between his comedies and his tragedies.

And to the music Feste contributes more than any other character. For "the Fool has an excellent breast" (II.iii.19f.), and though rightly a member of Olivia's household, must be borrowed by Orsino for the supply of his music. He is also, to use a good Elizabethan term, well-languaged. To recall a few of his sayings:

Foolery does walk about the orb like the sun, it shines
everywhere.   (III.i.39f.)

A sentence is but a cheveril glove to a good wit—how
quickly the wrong side may be turned outward!
                                              (III.i.11–13.)

No indeed, sir, the Lady Olivia has no folly. She will
keep no fool, sir, till she be married, and fools are as
like husbands as pilchards are to herrings—the husband's
the bigger. I am, indeed not her fool, but her corrupter
of words.   (III.i.33–37.)

I am afraid this great lubber, the world, will prove a
cockney.   (IV.i.14f.)

And thus the whirligig of time brings in his revenges.
                                                 (V.i.378f.)

But perhaps he is most brilliant in the conversation he
holds as Sir Topas the curate with the much-abused Malvolio in the dark house. For a brief extract:

FESTE. Say'st thou that house is dark?

MALVOLIO. As hell, Sir Topas.

FESTE. Why, it hath bay windows transparent as bar-
    ricadoes, and the clerestories toward the south-north
    are as lustrous as ebony; and yet complainest thou of
    obstruction?

MALVOLIO. I am not mad, Sir Topas. I say to you, this
    house is dark.

FESTE. Madman, thou errest. I say, there is no darkness
    but ignorance, in which thou art more puzzled than
    the Egyptians in their fog.

MALVOLIO. I say, this house is as dark as ignorance,
    though ignorance were as dark as hell; and I say, there
    was never man thus abused. I am no more mad than
    you are—make the trial of it in any constant question.

FESTE. What is the opinion of Pythagoras concerning
    wild fowl?

MALVOLIO. That the soul of our grandam might haply inhabit a bird.

FESTE. What think'st thou of his opinion?

MALVOLIO. I think nobly of his soul, and no way approve his opinion.

FESTE. Fare thee well: remain thou still in darkness. Thou shalt hold th' opinion of Pythagoras ere I will allow of thy wits, and fear to kill a woodcock, lest thou dispossess the soul of thy grandam. Fare thee well.[23]

Besides the music and the merriment which the Fool provides, the play has much excellent entertainment. As well as the delicately ironical scenes, full of lovely poetry, in which Viola confronts first Orsino and then Olivia, there are the scenes, less subtle, but no less entertaining to the groundlings—far more entertaining indeed—namely the drinking scene, the scene in which Malvolio is gulled with the forged letter, the scene where he appears before Olivia in yellow stockings, the mock duel between Aguecheek and the disguised Viola, and the scene with Malvolio in the dark house, from which I have just quoted—five scenes of first-rate fun, any one of which might have made the fortunes of the play with the general public.

Mirth and music, laughter and love—love tender and true with an adorable girl to represent it and love high fantastical in three distinct kinds—and all this so cunningly woven into the seamless robe of drama and so craftily dyed in the shifting colors of emotion as to defy analysis—it was a fitting play to celebrate Shakespeare's farewell to happy comedy.

When he came to the making of *Twelfth Night* he had nine comedies to his credit, to say nothing of the comic scenes and characters in *Romeo* and the Falstaff scenes in *Henry IV*; which means that by that time he possessed, at the back of his mind and ready to his hand, a heterogeneous collection of dramatic types, devices and characters, classical, medieval and Italo-Renaissance, which he could

23 IV.ii.35–62.

combine and *re*combine into an almost infinite variety of patterns.

All this, fused and transmuted in the crucible of his dramatic and poetic imagination, in the fullness of time produced that gem of his comic art, that condensation of life and (for those who know how to taste of it rightly) elixir of life—*Twelfth Night*. He could never better this—and he never attempted to. He broke the mold—and passed on!

Suggested References

The number of possible references is vast and grows alarmingly. (The *Shakespeare Quarterly* devotes a substantial part of one issue each year to a list of the previous year's work, and *Shakespeare Survey*—an annual publication—includes a substantial review of recent scholarship, as well as an occasional essay surveying a few decades of scholarship on a chosen topic.) Though no works are indispensable, those listed below have been found helpful.

1. Shakespeare's Times

Byrne, M. St. Clare. *Elizabethan Life in Town and Country*. Rev. ed. New York: Barnes & Noble, Inc., 1961. Chapters on manners, beliefs, education, etc., with illustrations.

Craig, Hardin. *The Enchanted Glass: the Elizabethan Mind in Literature*. New York and London: Oxford University Press, 1936. The Elizabethan intellectual climate.

Nicoll, Allardyce (ed.). *The Elizabethans*. London: Cambridge University Press, 1957. An anthology of Elizabethan writings, especially valuable for its illustrations from paintings, title pages, etc.

Shakespeare's England. 2 vols. Oxford: The Clarendon Press, 1916. A large collection of scholarly essays on a wide variety of topics (e.g., astrology, costume, gardening, horsemanship), with special attention to Shakespeare's references to these topics.

Tillyard, E. M. W. *The Elizabethan World Picture*. London: Chatto & Windus, 1943; New York: The Macmillan Company, 1944. A brief account of some Elizabethan ideas of the universe.

Wilson, John Dover (ed.). *Life in Shakespeare's England.*
2nd ed. New York: The Macmillan Company, 1913. An
anthology of Elizabethan writings on the countryside,
superstition, education, the court, etc.

2. Shakespeare

Bentley, Gerald E. *Shakespeare: A Biographical Handbook.*
New Haven, Conn.: Yale University Press, 1961. The
facts about Shakespeare, with virtually no conjecture
intermingled.
Bradby, Anne (ed.). *Shakespeare Criticism, 1919–1935.*
London: Oxford University Press, 1936. A small anthology of excellent essays on the plays.
Bush, Geoffrey Douglas. *Shakespeare and the Natural Condition.* Cambridge, Mass.: Harvard University Press;
London: Oxford University Press, 1956. A short, sensitive account of Shakespeare's view of "Nature," touching
most of the works.
Chambers, E. K. *William Shakespeare: A Study of Facts
and Problems.* 2 vols. London: Oxford University Press,
1930. An invaluable, detailed reference work; not for
the casual reader.
Chute, Marchette. *Shakespeare of London.* New York: E. P.
Dutton & Co., Inc., 1949. A readable biography fused
with portraits of Stratford and London life.
Clemen, Wolfgang H. *The Development of Shakespeare's
Imagery.* Cambridge, Mass.: Harvard University Press,
1951. (Originally published in German, 1936.) A tem-
perate account of a subject often abused.
Craig, Hardin. *An Interpretation of Shakespeare.* Colum-
bia, Missouri: Lucas Brothers, 1948. A scholar's book
designed for the layman. Comments on all the works.
Dean, Leonard F. (ed.). *Shakespeare: Modern Essays in
Criticism.* New York: Oxford University Press, 1957.
Mostly mid-twentieth-century critical studies, covering
Shakespeare's artistry.
Granville-Barker, Harley. *Prefaces to Shakespeare.* 2 vols.
Princeton, N.J.: Princeton University Press, 1946–47.
Essays on ten plays by a scholarly man of the theater.

Harbage, Alfred. *As They Liked It*. New York: The Macmillan Company, 1947. A sensitive, long essay on Shakespeare, morality, and the audience's expectations.

Ridler, Anne Bradby (ed.). *Shakespeare Criticism, 1935–1960*. New York and London: Oxford University Press, 1963. An excellent continuation of the anthology edited earlier by Miss Bradby (see above).

Smith, D. Nichol (ed.). *Shakespeare Criticism*. New York: Oxford University Press, 1916. A selection of criticism from 1623 to 1840, ranging from Ben Jonson to Thomas Carlyle.

Spencer, Theodore. *Shakespeare and the Nature of Man*. New York: The Macmillan Company, 1942. Shakespeare's plays in relation to Elizabethan thought.

Stoll, Elmer Edgar. *Shakespeare and Other Masters*. Cambridge, Mass.: Harvard University Press; London: Oxford University Press, 1940. Essays on tragedy, comedy, and aspects of dramaturgy, with special reference to some of Shakespeare's plays.

Traversi, D. A. *An Approach to Shakespeare*. Rev. ed. New York: Doubleday & Co., Inc., 1956. An analysis of the plays, beginning with words, images, and themes, rather than with characters.

Van Doren, Mark. *Shakespeare*. New York: Henry Holt & Company, Inc., 1939. Brief, perceptive readings of all of the plays.

Whitaker, Virgil K. *Shakespeare's Use of Learning*. San Marino, Calif.: Huntington Library, 1953. A study of the relation of Shakespeare's reading to his development as a dramatist.

3. Shakespeare's Theater

Adams, John Cranford. *The Globe Playhouse*. Rev. ed. New York: Barnes & Noble, Inc., 1961. A detailed conjecture about the physical characteristics of the theater Shakespeare often wrote for.

Beckerman, Bernard. *Shakespeare at the Globe, 1599–1609*. New York: The Macmillan Company, 1962. On the playhouse and on Elizabethan dramaturgy, acting, and staging.

Chambers, E. K. *The Elizabethan Stage*. 4 vols. New York: Oxford University Press, 1923. Reprinted with corrections, 1945. A valuable reference work on theaters, theatrical companies, and staging at court.

Harbage, Alfred. *Shakespeare's Audience*. New York: Columbia University Press; London: Oxford University Press, 1941. A study of the size and nature of the theatrical public.

Hodges, C. Walter. *The Globe Restored*. London: Ernest Benn, Ltd., 1953; New York: Coward-McCann, Inc., 1954. A well-illustrated and readable attempt to reconstruct the Globe Theatre.

Kernodle, George R. *From Art to Theatre: Form and Convention in the Renaissance*. Chicago: University of Chicago Press, 1944. Pioneering and stimulating work on the symbolic and cultural meanings of theater construction.

Nagler, A. M. *Shakespeare's Stage*. Tr. by Ralph Manheim. New Haven, Conn.: Yale University Press, 1958. An excellent brief introduction to the physical aspect of the playhouse.

Smith, Irwin. *Shakespeare's Globe Playhouse*. New York: Charles Scribner's Sons, 1957. Chiefly indebted to J. C. Adams' controversial book, with additional material and scale drawings for model-builders.

Venezky, Alice S. *Pageantry on the Shakespearean Stage*. New York: Twayne Publishers, Inc., 1951. An examination of spectacle in Elizabethan drama.

4. Miscellaneous Reference Works

Abbott, E. A. *A Shakespearean Grammar*. New edition. New York: The Macmillan Company, 1877. An examination of differences between Elizabethan and modern grammar.

Bartlett, John. *A New and Complete Concordance . . . to . . . Shakespeare*. New York: The Macmillan Company, 1894. An index to most of Shakespeare's words.

Bullough, Geoffrey. *Narrative and Dramatic Sources of Shakespeare.* 5 vols. Vols. 6 and 7 in preparation. New York: Columbia University Press; London: Routledge & Kegan Paul, Ltd., 1957–. A collection of many of the books Shakespeare drew upon.

Greg, W. W. *The Shakespeare First Folio.* New York and London: Oxford University Press, 1955. A detailed yet readable history of the first collection (1623) of Shakespeare's plays.

Kökeritz, Helge. *Shakespeare's Names.* New Haven, Conn.: Yale University Press, 1959; London: Oxford University Press, 1960. A guide to the pronunciation of some 1,800 names appearing in Shakespeare.

————. *Shakespeare's Pronunciation.* New Haven, Conn.: Yale University Press; London: Oxford University Press, 1953. Contains much information about puns and rhymes.

Linthicum, Marie C. *Costume in the Drama of Shakespeare and His Contemporaries.* New York and London: Oxford University Press, 1936. On the fabrics and dress of the age, and references to them in the plays.

Muir, Kenneth. *Shakespeare's Sources.* London: Methuen & Co., Ltd., 1957. Vol. 2 in preparation. The first volume, on the comedies and tragedies, attempts to ascertain what books were Shakespeare's sources, and what use he made of them.

Onions, C. T. *A Shakespeare Glossary.* London: Oxford University Press, 1911; 2nd ed., rev., with enlarged addenda, 1953. Definitions of words (or senses of words) now obsolete.

Partridge, Eric. *Shakespeare's Bawdy.* Rev. ed. New York: E. P. Dutton & Co., Inc.; London: Routledge & Kegan Paul, Ltd., 1955. A glossary of bawdy words and phrases.

Shakespeare Quarterly. See headnote to Suggested References.

Shakespeare Survey. See headnote to Suggested References.

Smith, Gordon Ross. *A Classified Shakespeare Bibliography 1936–1958.* University Park, Pa.: Pennsylvania State University Press, 1963. A list of some 20,000 items on Shakespeare.

5. *Twelfth Night*

Barber, C. L. *Shakespeare's Festive Comedy*. Princeton,
     N.J.: Princeton University Press; London: Oxford Uni-
     versity Press, 1959.

Bradley, A. C. "Feste the Jester," *A Miscellany*. London:
     Macmillan and Co., Ltd. 1929.

Brown, John R. *Shakespeare and His Comedies*. London:
     Methuen & Co., Ltd., 1957.

Charlton, H. B. *Shakespearian Comedy*. 4th ed. London:
     Methuen & Co., Ltd., 1949.

Evans, Bertrand. *Shakespeare's Comedies*. New York and
     London: Oxford University Press, 1960.

Frye, Northrop. "Characterization in Shakespearian
     Comedy," *Shakespeare Quarterly*, IV (1953), 271–277.

Furness, Horace Howard (ed.). *Twelfe Night, or, What You
     Will*. (New Variorum Ed.) Philadelphia, Pa.: J. P. Lippin-
     cott Company, 1901.

Hollander, John. *"Twelfth Night* and the Morality of In-
     dulgence," *Sewanee Review*, LXVII (1959), 220–38.

Hotson, Leslie. *The First Night of Twelfth Night*. London:
     Rupert Hart-Davis; New York: The Macmillan Com-
     pany, 1954.

Jenkins, Harold. "Shakespeare's Twelfth Night," *Rice In-
     stitute Pamphlet*, XLV (1959), 19–42.

Kermode, Frank. "The Mature Comedies," *Stratford-upon-
     Avon Studies III: The Early Shakespeare*, ed. John
     Russell Brown and Bernard Harris. London: Edward
     Arnold (Publishers) Ltd., 1961; New York: St. Martin's
     Press, Inc., 1962.

Knight, G. Wilson. *The Shakespearian Tempest*. New York
     and London: Oxford University Press, 1932.

Mueschke, Paul and Fleisher, Jeannette. "Jonsonian Ele-
     ments in the Comic Underplot of *Twelfth Night*," *Publi-
     cations of the Modern Language Association*, XLVIII
     (1933), 722–740.

Pettet, E. C. *Shakespeare and the Romance Tradition*. Lon-
     don: Staples Press, 1950.

Rich, Barnabe. *Rich's "Apolonius & Silla," an Original of
     Shakespeare's "Twelfth Night,"* ed. Morton Luce. New

York: Duffield & Company; London: Chatto & Windus, 1912.

————. *Rich's Farewell to Military Profession 1581*, ed. Thomas Mabry Cranfill. Austin, Texas: University of Texas Press, 1959.

Salingar, L. D. "The Design of Twelfth Night," *Shakespeare Quarterly*, IX (1959), 117–139.

Summers, Joseph H. "The Masks of *Twelfth Night*," *Shakespeare: Modern Essays in Criticism*, ed. Leonard Dean. New York: Oxford University Press, 1961.

Tilley, M. P. "The Organic Unity of *Twelfth Night*," *Publications of the Modern Language Association*, XXIX (1914), 550–566.